David James
(David Guthrie-James)

Escaper's Progress

D1146615

ESCAPER'S PROGRESS

ISBN 0–7117–0317–5

PRINTING HISTORY

Originally published as *A Prisoner's Progress* in Blackwoods
Magazine in December 1946 and Jan/Feb 1947.
In book form –
  1st Edition Blackwoods 1947
  2nd Edition Hollis and Carter 1954
  U.S. Edition (as *Escaper's Progress*) W. W. Noston N.Y.
  1955
  4th Edition Brown and Watson 1958
  Corgi Edition 1978
  This Edition David Guthrie-James 1986

This book is set in Intertype Plantin

Printed in Great Britain by Jarrold and Sons Ltd, Norwich. 186

Contents

PREFACE

WHEN it comes to acknowledgments, I have difficulty in knowing where to start, so many people there are to thank. Let me begin by mentioning Messrs. Hardy, Harrison and Cartwright, Evans, Hervey and Hugh Durnford, authors of the escape classics of the First World War. I read all their books at my preparatory school and was enthralled by their stories. It is the hope that a future generation of boys may be intrigued by my own escape that has induced me to add it to the list. Not only that, though. Both in spirit and technique, the above-named were the pioneers of escape, and it was largely their inspiration that helped so many of us to get away between 1939 and 1945. As long as there are wars there will be prisoners. Perhaps the boy who reads this book may find himself at some future date languishing in the hands of the Lilliputians, in which case my work, too, may be of interest and use.

Anyone who reads this book will find that there were many people in the camp without whose help I would never have got clear. Such men, for example, as George Beale, whose sympathy, help, and sound judgment were at everybody's disposal; Archie Cheyne and Johnny Pryor, always to the fore in any scheme, and both deserving to get away themselves; Lieutenant-Commander O'Sullivan and Billy Hussey, expert forgers – may they never turn their talents to £5 notes! – David Jolly, ex-C.I.D. man, whose journey along the Baltic coast gave me so much valuable information; and Frank Jackson, whose encyclopaedic knowledge of languages, inventive imagination, and ready wit not only got me home but also provided me with a trade name that will be remembered long after my own is forgotten.

Finally, my thanks to everyone in Marlag (O) for being such

staunch and cheerful friends in dark times. It is no mean achievement that all my memories of a prison camp should be pleasant ones.

D. J.

INTRODUCTION

by Eric Williams

SHORTLY after I arrived back from Germany in 1943, I was posted to a clandestine establishment in a country house not far from London where, it was thought, my recent experiences would be of value. It was there that I heard for the first time the fascinating story of a certain naval officer, explicitly named, who had bluffed his way from Marlag Nord to Sweden.

The fact that he had taken more or less the same route as we had done made his escape more than interesting to us. That he had made a prior escape in full Royal Navy uniform with the mere addition of a shoulder flash which read KRALOV BULGRSKI VOYENNO-MRSKOI FLOT or ROYAL BULGARIAN NAVY was a good joke against the Germans. That his papers had borne that unequivocal name we just could not believe; it seemed too good to be true. But such it was, as I discovered when I read David James's report.

This masquerade is in the direct tradition of the great naval escapes of the Napoleonic Wars. It has more affinity perhaps with the lighthearted escapes of the First World War than it has with the highly organized affairs of the latter part of the recent conflict. In this book you will find nothing of the Gestapo, nothing of torture or the threat of execution. Hardship and privation are here for they are the price the escaper is prepared to pay for his freedom, and how cheerfully David James puts down his money. The impression I gather from these pages is of a resourceful and likeable young man whose ready wit and pleasant manner proved a sound defence against rising suspicion. Time and again the reader feels 'This is it!' but, incredibly, the bluff succeeds, the forged papers are handed back and the Bulgarian officer is allowed to continue on his way.

9

David James was certainly lucky, every successful escaper owes his freedom to his luck, but he was also shrewd and full of guts. Above all he was a good loser, and when in the earlier escape attempt he was recaptured and reasonably treated this was, I can't help thinking, largely because he himself was reasonable and obviously expected to be treated so.

Escaper's Progress was written shortly after the war. Now, when the events of which it tells can be seen in their true perspective, I am certain that it will be enjoyed by everyone who believes in that indestructible British spirit which can be so clearly recognized between its pages.

CHAPTER ONE

CAPTURE

FROM early 1941 until February 1943 I was in M.G.B.s based at Felixstowe. It was a grand two years. I was fortunate enough to be in the flotilla of the greatest of the early Coastal Force leaders – that superb seaman, the late Lieutenant-Commander Robert Hichens, D.S.O. (bar), D.S.C. (two bars), and under his command there was never a dull moment. Nevertheless, I must resist the urge to write of those days, for they form part of a different story, and one already well told by Hichens himself in *We Fought Them in Gunboats,* and by Peter Scott in *The Battle of the Narrow Seas.*

During the first two months of 1943 life, for me personally, seemed to have reached a peak. My boat was working well, operations were plentiful and varied, friends used to come down almost every week-end from London to stay away from the air-raids, the duck were flighting with beautiful regularity into the salt marshes of the Orwell, and the pub close by was plentifully stocked with beer. Professional, social, and sporting life boomed, in fact, and there seemed no reason why the halcyon days should ever end. True, there was always the possibility of being knocked out, but in the armed forces it did not pay to consider possibilities like that. As for being captured, being suddenly cut off from this busy, happy life, that was obviously absurd.

Saturday, 27th February, 1943, was a busy day. My boat was inspected in the morning by a visiting Admiral. I was playing in a rugger match in the afternoon, and a relative was coming down to spend the week-end. At lunch-time I heard we were going to sea, so had to make some emergency arrangements. As soon as the match ended, a waiting taxi took me to the station, where I met my aunt. I just had time for a quick cup of tea; then, with a 'See you for breakfast tomorrow,' I was off. As I bade her farewell, I felt most strongly that I would not see her next day. This was the only time that I ever had such a feeling, and I have never been able to think of any explanation for it.

Our job that night was to escort a group of motor-launches on a mine-lay off the Dutch coast; thereafter we would have freedom of action until dawn. As soon as we were at sea, the sense of foreboding left me and I began to enjoy the first calm and warm night of the new spring. I even kicked off my thigh sea-boots in favour of a pair of shoes. This probably saved my life.

At 3 a.m., having already seen the M.L.s off home, our unit of four boats ran into a small German convoy just off the Hook of Holland. In the course of the ensuing battle my boat, which was built of wood and contained several hundred gallons of high octane fuel, was badly crippled and ultimately set on fire. Soon she was blazing from stem to stern, so we abandoned ship and swam about forty yards away, so that we and our rescuers, if any, should not be implicated if the tanks or depth-charges were to explode.

Almost at once, having seen our distress signals, 'Hich' and the two other boats returned. It was an extraordinary scene. The burning boat shed a vivid light over the whole area, while shadowy flak trawlers circled around in the wings. On this brilliantly illuminated stage, surrounded by the enemy, 'Hich' calmly stopped engines and started to pick up survivors. By the grace of God the enemy must have taken our rescuers for E-boats, for it was some minutes before they opened fire.

Treading water in the background awaiting my turn, I began to have high hopes of being saved, but it seemed to be a maddeningly slow business hauling chaps aboard in their thick water-logged clothes. Suddenly realizing who we were, the trawlers opened up again and 'Hich' had to move off. He had picked up six men in circumstances of some peril; it had been a wondrous effort. I can see him still, calmly standing on the canopy directing operations. Six weeks later, at the height of his powers and fame, he was killed.

The moment our rescuers left was one I had long been anticipating, but it was nevertheless heart-rending. Then, seeing a

Carley float with three men on it, I swam over and clung on. Almost at once, the boat commanded by Lieutenant John Matthias, R.N.V.R., gallantly returned for another attempt. He stopped rather far off, then swung on main engines to come alongside. When he was pointing in our direction the trawlers opened up again – he had to forge ahead in a hurry – the Carley float was swept aside. His bow hit my shoulder . . . bump, bump, bump, down the bottom . . . this was clearly IT, the three large screws couldn't possibly miss me . . . still, better to be killed outright than to drown slowly . . . hope I don't break his props or he'll have a job getting clear . . . a roar overhead . . . a double somersault like some bit of driftwood tossed by a mountain torrent, and the boat had passed me unscathed. I couldn't break surface in the confused water . . . took deep breaths to hurry things up. Shouldn't all the past incidents of life flash past a drowning man? I began to summon them up (rather self-consciously!) – home, family, sailing ballet, 'Hich', my boat . . . odd the way even in death one has the urge to play the right part . . . growing dimmer now, how easy it is to go – and how natural and unalarming . . . a pale watery moon appeared and I found myself on the surface. Thirty yards away a familiar voice was saying, 'Look, Jack, there's the skipper.' I turned, saw the Carley float, and with a final effort reached it.

Five minutes later a German trawler closed us. Mustering up my best schoolboy German, I shouted out: *'Helfen Sie uns, bitte.'* One of the crew said to me: 'Don't attract their attention, sir, or they'll shoot us.' This I refused to believe. Unlike land fighting or bombing, where passions are aroused, there is still a strong link between men of the sea. Each other they may have to fight in the course of war, but there is a common enemy – the elements. To all seamen worthy of the name a man in the water is a fellow-being in danger, and the colour of his skin doesn't matter. There is a further consideration. Owing to the very nature of their calling, seamen are more tolerant than other men, for it only needs travel to realize that, underlying rival political ideologies, there are good and bad in every country. For these reasons I refused to listen to my sailor's plea. Anyway, if this trawler didn't pick us up, no one else would. February is too cold for a prolonged swim.

She came alongside. Strong arms seized us and hauled us

aboard. It was good to feel solid deck underfoot again, but I was surprised when my legs folded up underneath me.

We were taken to the boiler-room – the warmest and most sensible place. Someone pointed at me and said, 'He is the worst.' My jerseys were pulled off and it hurt. Suddenly I realized that my temple and hand were both filled with shell fragments. Some strong coloured liquid was produced, and a packet of cigarettes. The doctor appeared and I was taken to his cabin. He cleaned and bound my wounds, saying they were not very serious. He then generously offered me his bunk. This I refused, saying I was too wet. In reality I wished to be with my crew to warn them not to talk.

Having seen to our immediate needs, the Germans left us alone. Stripping off our wet garments, we spread them over the gratings to dry, and ourselves on the drying garments to sleep. Our rest was but fitful, being constantly interrupted by the clang of engine-room telegraphs and the wail of the hooter. Evidently the ship had run into fog and was having difficulty working her way up the river.

For breakfast we were brought a large plate of brown bread and synthetic jam, followed by a bowl of unsweetened acorn coffee. An officer then came down, and, after asking us if we wanted anything, took particulars of our names and rank. He was surprised to find that I was an officer, since I was wearing an Iceland sweater and corduroy trousers, and ordered my immediate separation from the rest. I was taken to the tiller flat, where I spent the greater part of the day. My guards were lax and allowed me out to have a peep at Rotterdam, and I passed the time practising my rusty German on them. They seemed nice enough fellows, mostly of the merchant seaman type.

The mid-day meal was the only decent food I ever had from the Germans – *Wienerschnitzel*, plenty of well-cooked vegetables and a large plate of duff. After it, telling the sentry that my clothes were still wet, I succeeded in getting back to my crew. I told them that it was my intention to escape on the train, and that if I started to whistle a tune, they were to have a fight or create some other kind of diversion.

At four o'clock an escort with tommy-guns came alongside in a lorry. The captain came down to see us off, and on behalf of us all I thanked him for saving our lives. He replied simply that he was sure I would have done the same for him, and we shook hands. Our new guards insisted on searching us, and we were then taken to the station.

On the platforms and in the train we got many surreptitious winks and V signs from the populace. Between Rotterdam and Utrecht I feigned internal trouble and went continually down the corridor, but my captor was up to every trick of the trade. When I poked my head out of the window, his head was out further along the carriage. He smiled at me and twiddled a revolver round his finger. It was quite a comic scene. When I came out he gave me a cigarette as though to say, 'Now I know all your tricks, so don't play the fool with me or I'll have to be firm.'

We had dinner in Utrecht and caught another train. To my questions about where we were going, I was told Wilhelmshaven. In the train I had a compartment for my guard and myself. There were many fat Germans standing in the corridor, which struck me as an excellent joke. Later, back at home, I had to stand in the corridor for the benefit of a German P.O.W., and did not find it nearly so funny.

Our next stop was at Osnabrück, where we spent about four hours in a special waiting-room for prisoners, containing rough beds and blankets. Continuing our journey *via* Bremen, we arrived at Wilhelmshaven at about ten o'clock. Up to this point everything had been too new and interesting to leave much time for introspection. It was a curious little thing that brought our plight home to me. Wilhelmshaven Station was extremely like Felixstowe. There was the same layout of platforms and a very similar entrance. Suddenly I remembered that it was less than forty-eight hours since I had met my aunt at Felixstowe. Now I was several hundred miles away and there would have been no one to tell her and the rest of my family I was safe. This sudden cutting of all ties, like the curtain going down on a play, was the worst part of being captured.

We were met at Wilhelmshaven by a tall, dark Petty Officer, who asked me in good English whether we were able to walk. On hearing we could, he escorted us to a large barrack building about half a mile away. Here we were again searched and then locked in separate rooms. I threw myself on the bed and was soon fast asleep.

I was awakened at noon by being brought a large bowl of soup. I say a bowl; it was in reality a young basin. Its contents then and afterwards were always vegetable and very filling. For an hour one felt blown out, and after that very hungry again.

After lunch I was visited by the Petty Officer. His name, I gathered, was Grundmann, and he used, before the war, to come over to London and box for Hamburg against the Metropolitan Police. He had also spent two years in Brazil and about the same period in Australia. He was a fine type of man of the sort to whom one instinctively takes a liking. He was polite and friendly, but his promises were chiefly noteworthy for never being fulfilled. At this interview he said that the doctor would see me that evening; that he would arrange for me to have a bath next day, and that he would bring me some books at once. In fact, I saw the doctor next day, got a bath the following Thursday, and didn't see a book for a week.

All that afternoon I paced my cell, until at four o'clock I was summoned to see the Captain. Passing through a green baize door into another part of the building – ridiculously like going through from the forms and benches of the boys' part of the school to the master's more comfortable private house – I was taken into a well-furnished study. Sitting at a table was a fine-looking old man, stiff as a ramrod and with the appearance and bearing of a gentleman. Standing with his back to the fire was a shorter man, dressed as a civilian, with the high brow and thick spectacles of an intellectual. Feeling rather self-conscious, with two days' growth of beard, tousled hair and old clothes, I was introduced to Dr. Dietrich and Kapitän Ostermann as though I were an honoured guest. They ushered me to an armchair, offered me a cigarette, and told me to make myself at home. For an hour and more we, or rather Dr. Dietrich, talked. I have never discovered the object of that interview. He spoke at length of the happy days he had spent in England, usually as commentator at Wimbledon or other sporting events, then said how 'unhappy' the frightful tragedy of Dieppe had made him, how he had grieved to see ('with his own eyes') the flower of our manhood dead upon the beaches. He then had the arrant impertinence to shed crocodile tears over our misfortunes in the Far East, and reminded me that the Kaiser himself had warned the world of the yellow peril. Finally, saying, 'Well, Mr. James, we mustn't keep you from your supper,' he signified that this strange session was over.

Throughout the next day I paced up and down my cell, and by the late afternoon was quite looking forward to a further interview. Such is the effect of solitary confinement – a most powerful weapon.

Sure enough, at four o'clock I was again fetched, but this time taken to a study in a different part of the building, where the Captain sat alone at a desk with a typewriter. He evidently wished to take a statement and started from the very beginning. Feeling that it was better to canalize than repress the urge to talk, I gave him the maiden names of my grandmothers and the circumstances of my birth and early upbringing with the greatest readiness, and this, together with my preparatory and public school career, occupied the next two days and several sheets of foolscap. What interest such a commonplace and standardized boyhood can have held for the Kriegsmarine it is hard to say, but he banged it out on his typewriter with characteristic German thoroughness, continually looking up details in some old English directory so as to be able to append short descriptions of, say, Eton in brackets.

Throughout this time there was a packet of cigarettes on the table, from which I was told to help myself. I used only to smoke a little bit of each cigarette and put the rest in my pocket. Whenever my interrogator got up to consult one of his books of reference, I would quickly purloin a couple more. In this way I built up a little stock. I have since heard that everyone else under interrogation did exactly the same.

Finally, on my fourth interview, having left Eton, spent a year in a Finnish windjammer – her length, beam, and tonnage all included in the report! – and gone up to Oxford, we arrived at the outbreak of war. I then said firmly that there would have to be a gap in my biography from that date to the day I was picked up by the trawler. To my surprise he accepted this quite philosophically. He tried a few lines for getting more out of me, such as saying, 'Of course we know you were based at Felixstowe, or was it Lowestoft?' but on my maintaining a polite refusal to be drawn, he gave it up and started talking about Germany's grievances.

I could not but feel sorry for the old man. For twenty years,

he told me, he had lived in England, and his son was a natu-
ralized Englishman. It was hard to tell where his sympathies
lay, but at the age of seventy-three he had felt it his duty to
return and serve the land of his birth, and one had to admire
him for it.

This, though I did not know it, was to be my last interview.
For the next eight days I was just to sit in my cell.

It is hard to convey to anyone who has not experienced it
quite how demoralizing solitary confinement can be. My cell
was, I suppose, about twelve feet square and furnished with a
bed, table, and stool. My assets for self-amusement were one
shilling piece, which was all I had on me when picked up, and
one drawing-pin, which I found in the cell.

I was called with a bowl of acorn coffee at about eight
o'clock. I used to drink one cup of this, then use the remainder
for polishing the linoleum top of my table. For this purpose it
was quite admirable. Between eight and nine we were taken in
turns to wash. At nine o'clock came the big moment of the day,
when we were led out for half an hour's exercise. For this we
used to walk round a dismal quadrangle, with a grubby grass
centre, twice the size of a tennis-court. We were carefully spaced
out so as not to be able to talk, and any tendency to creep up on
the walker ahead, no matter how slowly it was done, was always
checked.

From our return to the cells at 9.30 there was nothing to do
till dinner at noon. The sole merit of this meal was that it blew
one out sufficiently to enable one to sleep for an hour after
lunch. From 1.30 I sat around till the evening meal at about 6
p.m. This meal was yet another vast bowl of soup and a hunk of
bread containing about six slices. If one wanted anything to eat
for breakfast it was necessary to keep some of this bread for
next morning. By the end of 'dinner' the day was as good as
over; that is to say, one had to do nothing for another two hours
before going to bed. I always managed to sleep for the full
twelve hours each night.

There were one or two particularly unpleasant things about
this régime. Worst was, of course, the lack of anything to do
and the consequent opportunity for brooding and self-cri-
ticism. It is a fact that every prisoner emerged from 'solitary'
convinced that he had made a mess of the action that led to his

capture. Secondly, despite the fact that my (not very severe) wounds healed quickly enough, I lost condition very rapidly on the German food. During my first fortnight in captivity I lost nearly two stone.

The only diversion was air raids. Hardly a day or night passed without the sirens going at least once, and when they did, we were all rushed with considerable noise and fuss down to the cellars. None of these raids came to much, but a few days after I left, the building was razed to the ground.

The chief problem was to find some way of passing the time. My first day was spent after the fashion of prisoners immemorial, in carving my initials upon the wainscoting of the cell. The only implement for this job was the milled edge of the shilling. Next day I had a stroke of luck, for I found an unsolved crossword puzzle, torn from an old English magazine, among the paper in the lavatory. I took it back to my cell and, lacking a pencil, scratched the answers in with the point of the drawing-pin.

One of my chief pastimes, till I grew too weak, was dancing Scottish reels and country dances. For the sword-dance I used a couple of stout straws from the paillasse in place of swords. Dancing a 'Sixteensome' with fifteen non-existent people (and a table in the middle!) was another favourite, as was going down an imaginary set in the 'Duke of Perth' or 'Hamilton House'. All this, I am aware, sounds idiotic, but one had to find something to do, or go mad.

In the evenings, or when I was tired of walking round and round my cell and dancing, I would 'go to the ballet'. The object of this unique aid to escapism (as opposed to 'escapology', with which later chapters will deal) was to whistle my way as far as I could through ballet scores, trying to visualize the action as I went along. In view of the fact that I had often gone to the ballet eight or nine times in a week on leave, I was depressed to find how difficult this was.

Although such expedients did help to pass the time, they were only efficacious because I knew that I would not be there for more than a few weeks. A prolonged period of solitary confinement would be terrible and I cannot understand how those who undergo it retain their sanity. A lively sense of humour and a vivid imagination are perhaps the most effective weapons with which to combat real boredom when it seems apparent that all the world has deserted one. One of the more important aids to passing the time is a clock or watch with which to see how quickly it passes. My own watch was lost when I was sunk, but I could see a church clock from the window. When we arrived it was stopped, but they obligingly got it going after a couple of days. It then kept perfect time, but was four hours twenty-six minutes slow. I had always previously imagined that double summer time was instituted as a sort of psychological sop. In reality I found it quite easy to get up at 3.34 a.m., have my lunch at 7.34 a.m., and go to bed at 4 p.m.

On the tenth day I was allowed some books. Most of these were 'Wild West' stories with half the pages out – nevertheless I read them twice; but one was more readable, W. H. Hudson's *A Shepherd's Life*. Thinking that what knowledge I had acquired about the 'drill' of the interrogation camp might come in useful to someone later on, I scratched a note in the fly-leaf:

> To whom it may concern: You will probably remain here for between two or three weeks, after which I am assured you go to a much better camp. Meanwhile, good luck, and if you want any breakfast don't eat all your bread the night before.
> (Sgd.) DAVID JAMES

For this gratuitous bit of information I was thanked by a new prisoner some six months later.

On the twelfth day things began to move. First was tried out the last expedient to get information. A man dressed as a civilian brought in a Red Cross form for me to fill up. It was an old German trick. Not only did the form require my name, rank, and the address of my next-of-kin, which are the Red Cross's proper interest, it also had spaces for the name of my base, the name of the captain, the number of operational flotillas there, and a hundred and one other naval details quite outside the scope of a charitable organization. The man displayed no resentment when I refused to fill in this crude trick document. Evidently he had failed with it too often before.

At noon I was brought not only my dinner but also a packet of sandwiches, and was told to be ready to leave immediately afterwards. About a dozen of us were fallen in, including my four seamen, and an officer and seven ratings from an L.C.T., taken about the same time as myself. To hear our chatter and laughter one would have thought that we were being repatriated. We had none of us talked to anyone except our captors since we were taken, and the relief was such as to make it one of the biggest days of our lives. We were marched two abreast to the station, prattling away nineteen to the dozen, and herded into the train. Still chattering for all we were worth – heaven knows what about – we left for Bremen.

On the way I was presented with the finest chance to escape. The guards were lax and very soon hung up their rifles or put them in the luggage rack. After a bit they even began going from our compartment to the next to see their friends. On one such occasion the train drew up at a small station. There was no one on the platform, the window was open, and I was unguarded. I thought for a moment and then turned the opportunity down. It was about forty miles to the Dutch border, over that marshy land that forms the lower reaches of the Ems. I had no maps and no compass, and was a conspicuous figure with hair unkempt, twelve days' growth of red beard, clad in rough sweaters, and with my head and hand bandaged. Certainly it looked a poor enough chance, but I now realize that I should have taken it; for, although miracles *do* occur to assist the escaper, they only happen to those who help themselves.

It must have been about five o'clock when we arrived at Bremen Hauptbahnhof. From there we were marched to the smaller Park Bahnhof, where we boarded an absurd little train which, as far as we could understand, ran a shuttle service on a small-gauge line to Tarmstedt, twenty-five kilometres away and near the camp to which we were going. The train was ridiculously understaffed. Having fussed into the station, it stopped for the guard to get out and collect the tickets. Meanwhile, the driver unhooked his engine and took it round to the other end of the train, then came back and clipped the tickets of the new passengers which had already been sold to them by the guard at the barrier. Finally, when all was ready, we moved off.

The effect of this procedure was to send us all into fits of laughter, much to the anger of the local populace, who presumably thought their train to be the last word in efficiency.

Running parallel to a main road, we were passed by all the trams, though it is fair to say that we managed to keep pace with a rather antiquated pony and trap. All this was to the symphonic accompaniment of the most extraordinary wheezes, groans, creaks, and bangs I have ever heard. The effect was strongly suggestive of a very ancient car going over a temporary bridge made of wooden boards.

It took this monument to George Stephenson exactly ninety minutes to go seventeen miles, and it was dark by the time we reached Tarmstedt. Worn out by overexcitement, rather like a child on Christmas Day, I failed to take stock of my surroundings, a failure that nearly cost me dear nine months later.

We were met by a German on a bicycle – an elderly naval officer called Schoof. Asking us in excellent English if we could all walk a couple of miles over very easy going, he was told that one rating had an injured leg. The wounded man was told that he could have the bicycle if the leg gave him any trouble, and we started off. So good were our spirits at the prospect of living with our fellows again that we sang all the way there. It was by no means the conventional entry to prison life.

After about half an hour's walk we could see the camp. It so exactly accorded with our ideas of what a prison camp should look like that our spirits rose even higher. A couple of dozen large blocks of wooden huts were surrounded by barbed wire. There were arc lights all round the perimeter and searchlights constantly playing over the surrounding fields. Not for the minute worrying whether it would be possible to get out of it, we agreed that it looked very picturesque.

Once inside the wire, we were taken into a large building, evidently a theatre. In front of a drop curtain a band was playing, and the walls were surrounded by ships' crests. After our experience of prison hitherto, it seemed pretty good to us.

The orchestra stopped as soon as we came in. One of them came over to me, produced – a packet of *Player's*! – and offered me one. Except for the Captain's French 'stinkers', this was my first cigarette for days. Somehow I had not thought to see English cigarettes again. My view of the place improved yet further.

Having filled in one or two forms of a harmless nature, we were searched yet once again and issued with 'tallies'. These were metal discs with the name of the camp – *Marlag und Milag Nord* – and our prison numbers on them.

The other officer and I were then taken by Schoof to the Officers' Compound, as we had been registered in the N.C.O.s'. Through a gate lay the barracks. A knock on a door and we were ushered into a room where a fair-haired Lieutenant-Commander sat making a model barge. After introducing us, Schoof withdrew; the naval officer opened a suitcase filled to the brim with cigarettes and gave us a packet apiece.

Explaining that since they had no warning of our arrival we would have to spend the night in the sick-bay, Lieutenant-Commander Jackson asked us if we felt like supper. When they took us to another block, we found everything prepared. In a room, which seemed warm and comfortable, sat several men in army battledress. They crowded round us asking innumerable questions about home, and then produced Welsh rarebit and cocoa from the stove. Again the result was to make us believe we had entered paradise and not purgatory; but the best was yet to come.

Gorged with food, chain smoking, and chattering to our new-found friends, we were taken down to the sick-bay. There we found spring-beds and – sheets! Once in bed, it took me long to get to sleep. It had been such a bewildering day that I hardly knew what to think.

In later times when I got so sick of it, it often made me laugh to think of that first night in the camp. I verily believe that I was happier then than on my first night of freedom in Stockholm.

CHAPTER TWO

CAMP LIFE

IT was a strange life into which we were precipitated. It took us three or four days to find our feet, and that we did so so quickly was largely due to the generosity and kindness of the older 'lags'. Within twenty-four hours of my arrival I found over a thousand cigarettes on my bed left by various anonymous friends.

The first morning we were taken to see the Paymaster. Much to our surprise he appeared to have a well-stocked clothing store. From it we were issued with army battledress, complete with shirts, collars, ties, boots, and all the other *etceteras.* Again, the generosity of friends was impressive. A number of people drifted in saying casually: 'Oh, I got a parcel last week; I've got quite enough already, so thought you might like a few extra handkerchiefs (or pyjamas, or razor blades).' On arrival in the camp my most treasured possession had been a piece of newspaper, folded to resemble an envelope, and containing a dozen cigarette butts (saved) and two cigarette papers (given me by a friendly guard). Now, within twenty-four hours I owned quite a substantial wardrobe.

We did not at first have to go through that period of reserve and suspicion which normally greets Englishmen in a new society. This was for two reasons: first, the kindness, already remarked upon; second, the fact that everyone was starved for first-hand gossip from home. For three days, therefore, we never stopped answering questions: What's the food like in England now? What's London like? Have you seen Edinburgh? What's the bomb damage in Plymouth? What were you in Coastal Forces? Did you know old So-and-so? Any news of repatriation?

At the end of that time the queries abruptly stopped. It was not out of rudeness. Simply the topic of conversation was finished. As one man said to me: 'You mustn't think me rude if I don't necessarily say anything to you in the mornings. You see, I've been here three years and my supply of small talk has run out.'

Unlike Britain, in Germany each Service looked after its own prisoners. Our camp was, on the whole, remarkably well run, since the personnel of the German Navy were a lot better than those of the other two Services. This was because the Navy was recruited from the Northern seaports – the old Hanseatic towns where interest was directed towards commerce and the outside world, and never to the canker that was within. A further factor was inter-Service rivalry. Ours being the only camp under Kriegsmarine jurisdiction, there is little doubt that they were keen to put up a better show than the Wehrmacht and Luftwaffe.

Marlag und Milag Nord was really two camps under a single command. Marlag, the Naval Camp, was to be my home for the next eleven months, Milag Nord was for the Merchant Service internees. Although it was but a few hundreds yards away, I never got up there. The only people who saw inside it were those in need of hospital treatment; for the camp contained a first-class surgeon in Major Harvey, R.A.M.C.

A small township with a population of between three and four thousand men of all colours and nationalities, it was, so I was told, somewhat suggestive of Barrie's *The Admirable Crichton* on a large scale, in that pre-war social values were completely reversed. Most of the Merchant Service officers were comparatively poor men. They received a little pay from the Germans, sufficient to buy odd things from the canteen, but that was their only source of income. The 'big shots', who could afford the best cabins, who had a couple of servants, and dined every night off chicken and Rhine wine, were the ex-stokers turned camp boxing champions, who fought for large purses; and the football stars, who commanded high transfer fees.

The richest man in the camp was, curiously enough, a Japanese steward. He was the most successful bookmaker, and had turned banker. His banking business was confined to cashing cheques. The special camp marks, valid only in camp canteens, issued to us by the Germans, were guaranteed to the Services by our own Government, because an equivalent sum was deducted from our pay at home. As regards the Merchant Service camp, the position was not so clear, nor was it certain whether the Government could be expected to convert into sterling fortunes of many thousands of marks won on the turf. The Japanese magnate, therefore, started his bank as a hedging bet. The official rate of exchange being fifteen marks to the pound, he discounted them at the rate of twenty-five. In this manner he made enough to be able to send over £1,000 home. People who went to Milag for an operation, and wanted to have a good time during their subsequent recovery, had only to see him and send an order to their bank in London with instructions to pay, say, £10 into his account, and he handed them 250 marks over the counter. The fact that by German rules we were not allowed to keep more than thirty marks in cash at any one time was, of course, irrelevant.

Unlike our camp, the profit motive was the mainspring of Milag. Every normal activity went on for gain. There were barbers, bootmakers, clothing stores, food shops, and other prosaic professions; there was also a choice of theatres every night. When the cinema was on, one would be shown to one's seat by a uniformed attendant. In the interval a sham theatre-organ would rise out of the pit, while a record of Reginald Dixon or Reginald Foort was played through the cinema amplifier. Everything was done to give people the illusion that they were at home.

The most popular pastime was the racing. I am not, quite frankly, clear over exactly what raced. I believe that the speed with which the 'horses' went round the track was dictated by dice, but in any case meetings were always well patronized, and large sums used to change hands after each event. There was a 'Tote', and an illuminated board which showed the number of the winner and the odds paid.

The black market was extensive and well organized. The Germans were very corrupt, and there was no known luxury that could not be obtained at a price, either for money or cigarettes. A friend of mine up there for treatment for a duodenal ulcer, saw a 10-lb piglet being thrown over the wire. He went to one of the *élite* cocktail parties, and was asked whether he would like champagne, Liebfraumilch, red wine, Schnapps, brandy, or the 'local special'.

This 'local special' was the product of another camp industry – the distillers. One evening, Lieutenant Rink, the second-in-command of the camp, an ex-Hamburg publican and up to his eyes in every sort of racket, happened to go into one of the galleys. He found it rigged up as a still, and was asked to give his professional view of the product. After tasting a glass, he said it was better – or anyway stronger – than anything to be obtained outside, but was there nothing to eat with it? On being told no, he went away, to return a few minutes later with a chicken under his coat. This was plucked and roasted whole on a spit ... and at 4 a.m. Herr Rink was carried, drunk, to the gate and deposited with the guard.

Over this camp, with its many nationalities, rather suggestive of some mining town in the nineties, presided Captain Nottman, the Senior Merchant Service Master. With no Naval Discipline Act at his back and no common Service tie of loyalty to support him, he must have been a man of strong character and great tact. Fortunately that is the type that the Merchant Service breeds, and he appears to have commanded the respect of British, Asiatics, and Germans alike.

Marlag was not at all like Milag, the chief differences being its smaller size and absence of the coloured element. The camp was divided into three sections. Going through the main gate one entered a German compound containing a large hut in which were lodged the guard company, offices, cells, and the parcel-room. To the left and communicating with it was a ratings' compound holding about 650 Chief Petty Officers, Petty Officers, and leading hands – seamen were sent to working camps elsewhere. On the other side was the officers' camp, which held, at the time of my arrival, about 150 officers with 50 orderlies.

It was a cardinal rule with the Germans to keep officers and ratings separate, presumably to make us a less effective force in the event of rebellion. It was, however, quite easy to evade this rule; for the camp dentist worked in the ratings' camp, and officers were taken over there under escort: so if one wanted to see anybody, one merely arranged a simultaneous appointment with the 'toothwright'.

In the officers' camp there were ten huts. Two of these, the lavatory and shower-room, were of brick; the other eight – the four living-huts, theatre, dining-room-cum-galley, sick-bay, canteen and classroom – were of a standard wooden type, double-lined throughout and reasonably warm and waterproof. Later, and from an escaper's point of view, the lavatory building was to prove of the greatest importance. It was divided by an inner brick wall into two, the one half being ours and the other half the German guards'. Their entrance was by a wired-in passage. It was thus possible to gain fairly easy entrance to the German compound by walking along the roof of this building.

The living-huts had long central passages with five large rooms on either side holding eight men apiece, and single rooms for senior officers at either end. The large rooms went by such names as 'Poets and Peasants', 'The Nut-house', 'Pot-Pourri', and so on; and in theory contained people who were fairly compatible. In practice there were bound to be occasional differences of opinion, though on the whole a surprisingly high level of agreement was maintained. The standard furniture provided by the Germans consisted of four double-decker beds, four double wardrobes, a table, iron stove, and eight chairs. These were arranged according to the taste of the occupants, together with what extras in the way of pictures, packing-case armchairs and sofas individual talent could produce.

I lived in 'Pot-Pourri', so-called because it contained one Norwegian, an American, a Dutchman, an Irishman (Liverpool variety), a Scot, and three Englishmen. Willy the Dutchman was our greatest character. With the usual industry and pertinacity of his admirable people, he never stopped working. If anyone was needed for digging the garden, peeling potatoes, or looking after the tomatoes, Willy would volunteer. If a lecture course was started in, say, archaeology or numismatics, Willy's shining morning face was certain to be in the front row. These 'extras' would, naturally, be additional to his usual studies of higher mathematics, languages, and the violin. With his English he took particular trouble, and became fluent in rather an academic way. When he was excited he sometimes reverted to type, and such classics as 'The gong is went' passed permanently into our speech.

One day Willy spent the whole afternoon learning his English proverbs. The next morning I wanted – I cannot conceive why – to get up early, so asked Willy, who was going to put in an hour gardening before breakfast, to call me. His face lit up, and he said, 'Of course. What is it your proverb says? The early bird beats the bush, isn't it?' To get recognizable fragments of three proverbs in six words must be a record.

The German Kommandant of both camps was Kapitän zur See Schuur, better known as 'Poop-deck Pappy'. He was a nasty little Prussian martinet, aged over seventy, with a white goatee beard. His manner was always scrupulously correct in a heavy and unendearing Prussian fashion. His only merit in our eyes was that he was doing his best to drink himself to death.

The immediate Kommandant of Milag was Kapitän Nibber, a sad-eyed individual of whom we never saw very much. Ours was Kapitän Bachausen, a short, fat, red-faced man known as Tubby. Of him it must be admitted that he was a gentleman and genuinely out to do the right thing. His fault was that he was so weak that nothing ever came of his efforts; he was completely dominated by Schuur.

A striking contrast to Bachausen was the Security Officer, Güssefeld. Always dressed in absurd leather riding-breeches, a pasty-faced, anaemic-looking sleuth, with a drip on the end of his nose, he was cordially loathed by everyone for his dishonesty, his oily, sneering manners, and his constant prying. Yet I am not sure that he was anything worse than efficient at a job naturally unpopular with us. We really detested him as the personification of our plight.

Our own Senior British Officer was Captain D. Graham Wilson, D.S.O., R.N. He had been out of the Navy for some years before the war and was a local magistrate. The S.B.O. of a camp had a most difficult hand to play, and for four years he played it with consummate skill. He always succeeded in getting the maximum out of the Germans consistent with the maintenance of our dignity. In this he was ably assisted by, first, Lieutenant-Commander Jackson, and then Commander Lambert, as 'man-of-confidence'. This, the worst job in the camp, meant being in close contact with the Germans in matters of common interest, such as drains, lighting, etc. By common usage and consent, the man-of-confidence was neutral, having no official knowledge of or part in escapes or other felonious activity.

The Germans left the internal organization of the camp to us. Except for counting us three times daily and having an occasional search, they did not come into the compound at all. The only exception to this was that two men called Joseph and Becker sat in an office in one of our barracks. What they did was never quite clear, but their presence made us more careful when we were engaged in illegal activity.

Camp routine revolved round three *appels* or roll-calls. Our cabin batman would come in with a bucket of hot water and draw the curtains at about 7.30. But for most of us the day started at five to eight (five to nine in winter-time), when the Duty officer went down the corridor shouting, 'Fall in for appel, please.' At this we would jump out of bed, pull greatcoat and trousers on over our pyjamas, and fall in on the parade-ground. There were inevitably a few strong-willed eccentrics who would be fully dressed, having had a cold shower. I myself never rose to such heights.

At eight o'clock Tubby would arrive in a decrepit hansom pulled by a white horse. The Feldwebel reported the numbers on parade and the numbers sick, provided, that is, that his incredibly foolish subordinates had succeeded in agreeing on a reasonable total. Tubby would then march down in front of the parade, beaming at us and saying, 'Good morning, Yentlemen' – his only English phrase – after which we would fall out and go to breakfast.

There is little doubt that if we had been dependent on German rations only, we should have died. All they gave us was a certain amount of inferior bulk – bread, potatoes, sauerkraut, beetroot, liverwurst with no liver in it, and a slab of horse carcase about once every ten days. For vitamins and luxuries we relied entirely on the very good parcels sent by the Red Cross. As one of the thousands who owe their lives to this wonderful organization, may I add my thanks to those of the rest. It is the only body in the world of which I have never heard any adverse criticism.

Unlike most camps, where every man drew his own parcel and then eked out the contents throughout the week as he saw fit, we had a system of general messing. This meant that the

Catering Officer, Lieutenant D. Woods, R.N.R., drew parcels for as many men as were on his books for the week and made out menus for the entire camp on the strength of their contents – a far more economical system.

On most days we had porridge, toast and marmalade with coffee, for breakfast. Lunch at 12.30 consisted of, say, corned beef and potatoes or soup, followed by bread and cheese. Then came two o'clock appel. Tea at 3.30 was accompanied by two slices of bread and jam. Finally, after six o'clock appel came a two-course supper, the big meal of the day. By ten o'clock most of us began to make a move for bed, and the lights went out at 10.30.

Such indeed is the skeleton of our daily life. How were the periods between meals filled in? As one would have gone mad doing nothing, most people managed to find themselves a job or hobby of sorts. Some of the more far-sighted prepared for their civilian post-war life, passing qualifying exams in banking, chartered accountancy, and so on. Others studied languages or higher maths. There was no branch of the Arts and Sciences which could not be studied, and the appropriate bodies – Royal Society of Arts, Institute of Bankers, and so on – could be relied upon to send out the right books and examination papers.

Many took their studies most seriously. One man in the camp worked ordinary office hours, nine to six, with Sundays free, half a day off once a week for a game of football, a week's holiday in August, and five days over Christmas. That was undoubtedly the best way to make the time fly, but was singularly hard to keep up; for though there were no distractions, there was no tangible stimulus to work and it was easy to slip back.

Besides the more serious studies, many light courses of lectures were arranged. By far the most popular of these was 'Law for the Layman' by an Australian barrister, but television, meteorology, and philosophy had their supporters.

An immense amount of ingenuity was put into the theatre. It had been built as an ordinary hut, but not partitioned off into rooms. The Germans provided the wood and materials for our carpenters to do the work, and the result was said to be the second best camp theatre in Germany. The official opening was celebrated by a production of *The Wind and the Rain* the day after I arrived, and provided me with another excellent reason for being so impressed with the place. The auditorium was tiered and could seat about 160. The stage, though small, was built on modern lines, with dimming switches, coloured footlights, and so on. Finally, there was a deep orchestra pit which could hold our twelve-piece orchestra.

On this stage a play was given about once every two or three weeks. There were four men keen on production and they used to take it in turns. During my year in the camp they produced such plays as *Banana Ridge, Night must Fall, French without Tears, Busman's Honeymoon, Rope,* and *Ten Minute Alibi.*

Apart from providing entertainment for the players and audience, this gave endless work to the long-suffering camp carpenter, Lieutenant-Commander 'Nobby' Clark, and his staff. As soon as one show was over, plans for the *décor* of the next would be ready. Flats would then have to be painted and furniture made from what scraps of wood were available. Even more heroic were the labours of another ex-submariner, Lieutenant Boulnois, R.N., who designed and executed the costumes. The only respite he had was when the play under rehearsal demanded dinner jackets, for these could be made easily enough by pinning silk to the lapels of naval uniform and covering the buttons. Suits could usually be hired from the Germans 'on parole', but it was the leading ladies who gave the greatest difficulty. Providing suitably rounded costumes to fit the somewhat angular beauties of Royal Marine and Naval impersonators was a task to give anyone a headache.

Besides the plays, a further job for the theatre staff was organizing the weekly concerts. These were alternatively band and gramophone. Our orchestra, led and trained by Houston Rogers, the theatrical photographer, practised many hours a week. In fact, to anyone living near the music-room it seemed doubtful if they ever stopped practising. Few of them had played any musical intruments before they were captured, but within their limits they became very good. These limits were jazz and light orchestral music. In their more ambitious moments they tried Beethoven, but were foiled by the inadequacy of the strings. Our violinists were excellent if supported by three saxophones, three clarinets, a piano, drums, and an oboe to drown the mistakes, but they could hardly compete un-

34

aided. It was 'Smuts' Rogers himself who made the orchestra. One of those fortunate people who can play anything from harp to penny whistle, he was a born showman and his concerts were always a rousing success.

The orchestra was equipped with a double-bass, which exemplifies the astonishing ingenuity of prisoners. Since one was badly needed, Nobby Clark set to and made it out of odd bits of packing-cases, paper, and glue. It proved to be a most adequate bass accompaniment. Encouraged by this, he then made a 'cello! The gramophone concerts afforded another example of his way of tackling problems. With only ordinary portable gramophones available, it was hard to give a concert which 160 people could hear satisfactorily. A wooden frame was therefore made, and over it was stretched varnished paper. With this as an amplifying horn, the standard H.M.V. was clearly audible in every part of the hall.

Besides concerts and plays, the theatre was also used for cinemas, discussions, and talks. We were given a talkie apparatus by the Y.M.C.A., who used to come round about once a fortnight showing German light (usually not so light) musical comedy films, with English captions. We had a discussion group called Marlag Forum, which held meetings fortnightly. Finally, there was a series of lectures on recent naval events, usually given by participants. So as not to arouse the interest of the German censor, these were billed under the most innocent names; for instance, 'Plymouth Hoe', by Lieutenant-Commander Beatty, V.C., was the story of the St. Nazaire raid. To allay any German inquisitiveness during the lecture, there was a gramophone on the stage. If the look-out gave warning, the lecturer had to break off his description and say, 'My next record will be "Mairzey Doats".' It was all so incongruous as to be funny, except for the unfortunate speaker, who, suddenly cut off in the middle of his talk, never knew whether to stand by the gramophone or leave the stage.

The sports were well run. The great stand-by was soccer, which went on practically the whole year round. This was usually run on leagues lines, with a dozen teams calling themselves Arsenal, Chelsea, and the like, picked to be as equal as possible, and playing each other twice for a points system competition. There was also a cup-tie knock-out, with a good deal of enthusiasm and even ill-feeling generated as Cup Final Day approached. As soon as one league was finished, there was a re-draw, a re-hash of the rules to allay criticisms of the last contest, and the whole thing would begin over again. There were also periodic 'internationals' – it was grand to hear a good Glaswegian cheer of 'Come on, Scotland!' in the very heart of Germany – and sometimes other representative games such as 'Elderly Gentlemen v. Venerable Veterans'.

The only trouble with our football ground was that it was covered with flints and sand. This did not worry the soccer enthusiasts much, but was hard on the rugger fans and crick-eters. Rugger was, in the end, limited to ten-a-side touch rugger, a fast game for which, in our underfed conditions, twelve minutes each way was more than enough. We were able to have only a short cricket season of some three weeks, for the balls soon gave out. Even this had to be played on a matting wicket with bowling from one end only. The German guards used to get quite a few cigarettes retrieving sixes.

So much for the public and organized activities of the camp. The participants themselves were of interest, for they were rep-resentative of most of the naval disasters of the war. It took one back a long way, for example, to meet the two officer survivors of the *Rawalpindi*, which was sunk north of Iceland in 1939. There was one from the *Glorious*. The majority had been taken from two armed merchant cruisers sunk early in the war – *Voltaire* and *Vandyck*, names familiar to many who had done a Baltic or West Indian cruise, and known to us, facetiously, as 'V-Class Battleships'. There were also survivors from four of the early submarines – *Seal*, *Sharp*, *Undine*, and *Starfish*. Quite a number were from Crete, St. Nazaire, and Dieppe, but subsequent to that only one or two came to us, and those, like myself, were from Coastal Forces, captured in the Channel.

CHAPTER THREE

ESCAPE – THE PROBLEM

THERE was one other camp hobby with which I have not
dealt hitherto. That was escaping. The main drawback to this
fascinating pastime was that it rendered any other constructive
activity impossible; for, quite apart from the great amount of
work involved in preparation, it was psychologically out of the
question to settle down to do tomorrow's Spanish 'prep' if there
was a chance that one might be making a dart for it that night.

Long before, in my prep-school days at Summerfields, I had
read all the escape classics of the last war – such books as *The
Tunnellers of Holzminden, Within Four Walls, I Escape,* and
The Escapers' Club – and as a proposition the business of escaping fascinated me.

During my first few weeks in the camp I did much abstract
theorizing on the subject. At first I was of the opinion that the
ideal was to concentrate on never being seen at all from the
moment one left the camp till the moment one arrived in a
neutral country. This theory soon developed a more subtle in-
terpretation. 'The best place to hide a leaf is in a wood,' the old
saying goes, and this I adopted as a motto. Its application to
escaping meant that the best method would be to assume some
everyday character-part, mix with the crowd, and stay there.

Once on this line of thought, I came to the conclusion that
the perfect escaper would have been that famous practical joker
of Edwardian days – Horace de Vere Cole. He perpetrated the
well-known stunt of roping off a bit of Piccadilly, digging it up
and then leaving it. He it was, too, who impersonated the
Sultan of Zanzibar and reviewed the Home Fleet. There were
several other jokes of a similar nature that he played while still
an undergraduate at Cambridge, and the lesson to be drawn
from them all was that it is possible to get away with anything

37

as long as it is done with sufficient *audacity* and without hesitation.

The human mind seems to be inherently lacking in suspicion. Many incidents have come my way to prove this. A friend of mine was once Officer of the Watch aboard a destroyer in dock in Glasgow for Navy Week. In the next berth lay a cruiser, her deck and bridge a moving stream of humanity being shown or shoved round by perspiring Petty Officers. Without much interest, my friend noticed a little man in a bowler hat sitting up on the cruiser's range-finder, evidently at work. After a bit he sent a signal across to his opposite number, saying, 'Is man on your range-finder authorized?' By the time an investigator had gone up there, the man had disappeared, taking with him £70 worth of prisms from under the very noses of both Navy and tax-payer.

Such instances abound, and the gullibility of the human mind has often saved escapers. One of the best known, Gordon Instone, reported that on a certain railway station he was driven by Gestapo attention to take refuge in what appeared to be a station waiting-room. Imagine his horror when he discovered that it was in reality a Mess, full of German officers. Quickly gathering his wits, he did not retire with mumbled apologies as most of us would, but went boldly over to the electric light switch, took it to pieces, and put it together again. Naturally, nobody thought an electrician would enter without permission, and he was able to leave by another door.

Another escaper took refuge in the house of a priest in France. While the priest was out he heard banging on the door, and a glance at the window showed a German sentry there. Did he try to hide? No. He went and opened the door. 'Where is the priest?' said the German officer standing outside. 'Gone to a sick case.' 'Please convey my apologies, but we have information that there are escaped prisoners in the neighbourhood. Since this is the biggest house in the village, we propose to carry out a practice search.' Leaving the escaper sitting by the fire, the Germans carried out a meticulous search of the house – in cupboards, under beds, and on the rafters. Returning to the prisoner, the officer clicked his heels and said, 'Heil Hitler! Will you please thank the priest and tell him we are now confident that we would find nobody rash enough to hide in his house.' And so, no doubt, they would, unless he were sitting under their very noses.

Even sentries on prison camp gates have an astonishing tendency to take people at their face value. There can be few camps that did not, at some time or other, get people out disguised as neutral commissions, foreign workers, washerwomen, and the like. The best effort in that line I ever heard came from VII B, a camp near the Swiss border, from which a 'German General' left with his whole staff. The 'General' himself, a Colonel Blimp type of soldier, actually spoke no German, but his 'Adjutant' had lived for many years in Munich. Perfectly dressed by the camp tailoring staff, the General, his A.D.C., and four others approached one of the two main gates just after a change of guard. The sentry almost dropped his rifle to see a live General, but succeeded in presenting arms. The Adjutant then roared out to him to call out the guard, and it was duly inspected by the General. After a whispered conversation the Adjutant announced that as the General had laryngitis he would not address the troops in person, but wished them to know that he was horrified with their slack and slovenly appearance. And where was his car? Nobody, of course, knew. Never mind, said the General, he would walk; so the little party set off, leaving the Germans quivering with fear. Unfortunately, the Feldwebel, to forestall the court martial, which by this time he regarded as inevitable, rang up the Kommandant to explain that he had not been told the General was coming. Neither, for that matter, had the Kommandant, and in an agony of apology he gave chase in his car. Alas! He recognized one of the little party, so they returned in less splendour than they had left!

There can be little doubt that the Germans are the most gullible people in the world, but lest it should be thought that such imbecility can exist only in Germany, let me admit that the coolest customer, the most acute psychologist of all escapers in the last war, was Baron von Werra of the Luftwaffe. He escaped from a camp in England and promptly rang up the police! To them he explained that he was a Pole who had force-landed in the neighbourhood and was about to go to the nearest R.A.F. station. He then rang up the R.A.F. and repeated the same story, having the nerve to ask them to send down transport for him. While he was being fetched the Intelligence Officer rang up the police, who said, 'Yes, we know all about him.' So he got off to the best possible start.

On arrival he was taken to see the Intelligence Officer, where, claiming that he came from some obscure station in Scotland, he played to the very limit the bluff that his squadron would be so worried over his absence, could he ring through and let them know that he was safe. There was a delay on the line – that was a safe bet in early 1941 – and so Von Werra asked if he could have a wash and brush-up. He was told to go down the passage, first on the right; but no sooner had he gone out than the Intelligence Officer thought it would be best not to let him out of sight till his identity was established. He was just about to follow when Von Werra poked his head round the door and said, 'Excuse me, did you say first left?' That set the other's mind at ease, for if it were a blind, why should he care which side the door was on?

Half an hour later the call came through. No such Pole existed. The Intelligence Officer hurried along, only to find that his man had gone. He was ultimately found at the far end of the aerodrome, warming up a Spitfire! He deserved to get away with it too.

As a result of this exploit he was sent post-haste to Canada; a letter was also sent saying that he was dynamite and should be treated as such. Unfortunately it was delayed in the post, and by the time it arrived Von Werra had already crossed the border into neutral U.S.A. It is sad to relate that he was subsequently killed on the Eastern Front. He was by all accounts a sincere patriot and very decent fellow.

Yet another example of the way everybody takes the things under his nose for granted was the superb 'Trojan Horse' escape from Sagan. This will undoubtedly go down to fame as one of the classic escapes of all time.

It remained, however, for Milag to provide the perfect happy-ending romance of escape. There was a certain Merchant Service officer called Richard Bird. In the spring of 1939 he became engaged to a girl in Oslo. In 1940, when the Germans walked in, they lost contact with each other. In 1941 Bird's ship was torpedoed by a raider in the Pacific; he was picked up and put aboard a blockade runner, which successfully got back to Germany, where he was incarcerated in Milag. In the autumn of 1943 he succeeded in making good his escape and reached Stockholm. A message was got through to his fiancée in Oslo. She, too, managed to slip out of the German grasp; the British colony in Stockholm produced a wedding dress; they were duly married and ultimately flown home together. In the height of a war which dashed so many hopes of happiness, one cannot but derive comfort from a story such as this.

At that time, however, none of these stories was known to me, and the concrete problem of how to break out was still unsolved. It certainly was rather a poser. Situated in flat, sandy country, the camp was entirely surrounded by two barbed-wire fences about ten feet high and six feet apart, with rolled concertina wire between them. At each corner there were raised 'tiger boxes' fitted with search-lights and 'hurry-up' guns. There were also arc-lights, and sentries posted all round the perimeter. It would probably take the best part of a quarter of an hour to cut through this barbed-wire entanglement, and that without a vestige of cover and within a few yards of sentries. It was hardly an attractive proposition.

As a result of finding a tunnel in the summer of 1942, the Germans had taken effective precautions. These included microphones at thirty-yard intervals round the wire to detect the noise of digging. They had whitewashed the earth under the raised barrack floors, too, and they carried out regular inspections to see whether there were traces of shafts or soil disposal.

To get out of the camp would be hard, and the problem was by no means solved once one was clear. It lay in a densely populated military area, and it would be essential to escape in such a manner as to get right away from the area before absence was discovered. Thus, slipping away from a working party, which would lead to discovery within half an hour, was completely out. The camp had had a long run of bad luck in escaping and it was generally agreed that the Kommandant was right when he said that nobody would ever escape from his camp. 'It was too near England.'

Probably nothing had been a greater setback than the fiasco of the 1942 tunnel. A beautiful piece of work, it was over a hundred feet long and had caused its constructors infinite hard

41

toil. About forty officers were scheduled to go from it, but by sheer ill-fortune a prowling sentry with a dog stumbled over the sixth man as he poked his head through the hole.

The first out, a Frenchman called René Barnett, serving with the British Navy, got by train as far as Cologne, where he was spotted by a sharp-eyed Gestapo man. Numbers two and three, Lieutenant Trevor Beet, R.N., and Lieutenant 'Johnny' Wells, R.N.V.R., knowing nothing of the disaster behind them, walked ten miles south across country, only to run into a waiting patrol at the railway station they had selected. The same fate befell number four, Lieutenant M. ('Wicked') Wynne, D.S.C., R.N.V.R., the man who torpedoed the lock-gates at St. Nazaire.

Only the last man, Lieutenant Tommy Catlow, R.N,. had any luck. He heard the outcry as his partner was caught just behind him, but carried on, not with any hope of getting clear, but in order to draw a red herring across the trail of those ahead. After a couple of nights' walking he found himself in Hamburg. Suffering from sore feet, he went into a shop and bought some sticking-plaster. He then caught a train up to Flensburg on the Danish border, and, disembarking, succeeded in getting well into Denmark on foot. Here fortune deserted him. Worn out, he went up to a farm for help – and it turned out to be the one German farm in the neighbourhood. Nevertheless his journey had accomplished much. He had proved that, given the luck, it was possible to get out of the district. The sticking-plaster episode, too, showed that doing the 'everyday' things was not suspicious, and that there were so many foreigners about that lack of German was no longer a cause for comment. These things, it is true, may have been known in other camps, but we were such isolated entities that each camp had to gather its own experience.

To sum up, I came to the conclusion that escaping was essentially a psychological problem, depending on the inobservance of mankind, coupled with a ready acceptance of the everyday at its face value. The matter could be subdivided into four separate questions. First was getting out of the camp – a real 'stinker', which could be tackled either by the guile approach (disguise, hanging underneath a lorry, and so on), by tunnelling, or by cutting a hole in the wire. Second was the getting out of the area, the *pons asinorum* of the whole business; and which-ever way one looked at it, that largely depended on luck. I was then of the opinion, and hold it even more strongly now, that once safely in Bremen one was a good three-quarters of the way home. Third was the passage from Bremen, across Germany, to the point of departure from the country. This should be quite easy, and would depend only on good routeing, good planning, and meticulous attention to detail. Finally, there was the actual escape from the country. On this we hardly had enough infor-mation to theorize, but it was obvious that both skill and luck would be needed.

One more point – it was clear that care and forethought would play their parts. It was even more clear that luck would play a greater one. Luck is the most essential part in an escape. No successful escaper will disagree with that, though there is some controversy whether it is the luck of the roulette wheel and the law of averages, or the 'luck' which can be ascribed to Providence. I have now read the story of every successful escape from Germany in this last war. I doubt very much whether any total duds got away, but I am quite certain that for every man out, there were at least ten better men would have got clear but who did not have the good fortune they deserved.

CHAPTER FOUR

'MABEL' – AN ANSWER

THERE was in the camp an officer called Rodwell, who was something of a character. An electrical specialist, aged about forty-five and with a great love of adventure, he had been captured from my flotilla while out joy-riding one night. Mad keen on escaping, he was the moving spirit behind most of the attempts made during the year I was there. His great drawback was his incredible look of guilt. 'Roddy' taking out a packet of mustard and cress to sow in the garden looked about as innocent as Guy Fawkes bound for the House of Commons. We always said he should have been dressed in a black cloak and tall hat, with a dagger at his waist.

As soon as I arrived in the camp, Roddy asked if I should like to join him in a scheme to get out. A glance at the plan on pages 22–3 will show that there was one stretch of the wire on either side of the main gate leading out of the German guards' compound which was only a single fence. To get through this would need only four cuts instead of about fifteen. The idea was to choose a really dark night and then climb over into the German compound *via* the roof of the lavatory block, crawl round the back of the guard-house, and cut our way out there. Our plans for when we were once free were somewhat vague, but we were equipped with passes to show that we were French workmen, and we hoped to make our way to the Dutch border.

The moonless period at the end of March was chosen, and one dark night we tiptoed over to the lavatory. After a few minutes we realized that conditions were not suitable. As soon as our eyes got used to the darkness we found that we could see quite far, and it was one of those dead-quiet nights when sound travels for ever. Half an hour after leaving our hut we were back in bed, and so ended my first escape effort. It did but whet

44

Roddy's appetite, however, and for nights afterwards he was to be heard jumping in and out of bed to take advantage of any spell of dark cloud. One night he earned our righteous indignation by waking us all up to tell us that it wasn't as dark as he thought it was!

It was after this abortive episode that I gradually adopted the idea of travelling by train, so I spent the next two months working very hard at my German. In order to get plenty of practice, I undertook most of the camp Black Marketing activities. The cigarette ration of our guards was three a day, and they would do almost anything for more. We received fifty a week from the Red Cross and as many as we liked from home. Some people had a store of several thousand in suitcases under their beds. We therefore did quite a lot of trading. This was, in my view, a good thing. Quite apart from the welcome little luxuries we were able to obtain, it helped to give the lie to Goebbel's propaganda about starving Britain and enabled us to keep the guards under our thumb. And I was soon able to assess the degree of corruption of each individual guard, and decide whether he was the right man to ask for torches, wire-cutters, or other contraband items.

As a matter of interest the following was our scale of prices for the more common transactions:

Eggs – 8 cigarettes each.
Onions – 20 cigarettes per lb.
Cigars – 5 cigarettes each.
Matches – 2 cigarettes per box.
Pocket-knives – 30–100 cigarettes.
Champagne – 250 cigarettes per bottle.
Schnapps – 200 cigarettes per half-litre.
Cigarette lighters – 20–100 cigarettes.

At various times we obtained in addition such goods as paint-boxes, violin strings, apples, cider, sweets, chickens (dead), rabbits (alive), razors, razor-strops, fountain-pens, sunglasses, brief-cases, face-cream, and even a calf-skin for a new drum!

By far the most corrupt German was the interpreter, Henry Schieman. Like many others, he went to America in the twenties and became a small-time gangster. Foolishly accepting the offer of a cheap cruise back to the Fatherland, he arrived in Hamburg to be put straight into uniform. It was one of Hitler's silliest moves. Most of the men enticed back in this manner held interpreters' jobs, and all bore a grudge against the régime. Henry could be relied upon to give us warning of any camp search. He was also responsible for 'frisking' recaptured escapers, and provided he was told what one really treasured, he never turned it in to his own people.

Money was obtained from the guards, but not for cigarettes. As I have explained, we were paid by the Germans in special 'camp marks' at the rate of fifteen to the £, and these were guaranteed to us by our Government at that rate. Many of our guards had vivid memories of inflation after the previous war, and were therefore prepared to do a straight exchange of Reichmarks for lagermarks as a hedging bet, and in the hopes that they would be able to obtain sterling from the British Government at the same rate.

There was in the camp an Escape Committee whose job it was to co-ordinate escapes and to help those who wished to get away. We had a system of 'patents', whereby if anyone had a scheme for getting out, he 'registered' it with the Committee. He had to do this to get the Captain's permission to 'leave the ship'; also he thereby ensured getting the first crack at his own idea. The Committee consisted of a representative from each of the barracks, all of whom had made escape attempts, presided over by Commander G. H. Beale, R.N. Attached to them was a staff of 'experts', including forgers, tailors, and an Intelligence Officer, who kept up to date the Escape Book in which were written details of the various escape routes, reports brought in from other camps, and such information about trains as we could pick up from the guards and daily papers.

Early in June a scheme for a tunnel was advanced by Lieutenant-Commander Archie Cheyne, R.N. A glance at the plan will show that the mess-hut ran parallel with the north wire and about twenty-five yards from it. This hut was half dining-room and half galley, the two halves being separated by a partition, and for constructional reasons this partition was supported by a brick wall on which the floor joist rested. There were some piles of bricks in the camp at that time, and the proposal was to put up a dummy brick wall three feet from the original, in the hopes that in that confined space the Germans might not notice that it was suddenly only fourteen feet instead of seventeen feet from their inspection hole.

This plan was adopted, and some forty volunteers accepted for duty, while Archie Cheyne himself, a tunneller of considerable experience, was put in charge of the work. As usual, the German 'ferrets' (as we called the regular search-party) inspected the ground under all the huts on Saturday morning, and by the following evening our brick wall, cemented with putty, was in place, giving us a splendid chamber twenty-five feet by three feet wide and about three feet six inches deep in which to sink the shaft of tunnel and store the day's excavations. The entrance was under the porch of the dining-room, and the trap-door was well camouflaged by a removable wooden grating and the mud people normally brought in on their feet.

We were faced with the usual prison-camp security dilemma. It would have been impossible to conceal from our fellow-prisoners the fact that a tunnel was being dug underneath their breakfasts, and any attempt to do so would only have led to inquisitive gossip. On the other hand, we had no wish to broadcast our plans. After some discussion, we felt it would be better to tell everybody what was going on. As 'tunnel' is the same word in German as in English, it was agreed, if we must discuss progress among ourselves, to call it *Mabel*. The tunnel of the year before had been known as *Lucy*.

Roddy was in charge of the electrical side, and was soon in his element. No. 9 hut was at that time empty. Looking incredibly villainous, he broke in one evening and stripped it of fittings. Half an hour later, he emerged with some 200 feet of wire wrapped round his middle. Lamp-shades were made out of pint bottles with the bottoms snapped off and the leads running through the neck. Breaking the bottom off the bottles was an ingenious operation. A piece of wool, soaked in petrol, was wound tightly round the bottle and set on fire. After burning for a minute it was plunged into cold water, when the sudden change in temperature usually resulted in a clean break. Main lighting in the chamber under the dining-room, and at twenty-feet intervals down the tunnel, was operated by a switch from the chamber itself, so that it could be used for signalling to the face. There was also a red warning light controlled by a revolving hat-peg in the dining-room. Whenever work was in progress there was a look-out there to warn the diggers if the 'ferrets' came into the camp.

One of our main worries was the microphones. The tunnel was planned to pass midway between two of them, and stringent orders were given for as much silence as possible, but this was not felt to be enough. It was therefore arranged that a hard-tennis court should be made in the space between the dining-room and the wire to act as a cover for any noise made. Two men were always at work here, levelling off a bit of perfectly flat ground and banging in bits of stone and rubble to create as much percussion as possible.

We worked in four watches of six. This meant doing no more than a shift every second day, but the air in the tunnel got very foul, and it was good policy to keep the men who would be going out as fit as possible. The morning shift was from 9.15 till 12.15, and the afternoon from immediately after two o'clock appel till 4 p.m.

No. 1 of the team worked at the face, the most interesting job, but rendered unpleasant by foul air. No. 2, immediately behind him, shovelled the earth into bags made of sewn blankets, then gave a tweak on a rope made of plaited strips of blanket, and the bag was hauled back and an empty one sent up in its place. Originally this haul was made in one, but at eighty feet there was so much stretch in the rope that a half-way house had to be inserted and the haul split into two. In this middle gallery sat No. 3, busy passing bags both ways. No. 4, at the bottom of the shaft, was a galley-slave pure and simple, hauling back bags and passing them up the six-foot shaft to No. 5, who with No. 6 had the easy job of emptying them on the disposal dump.

Perhaps it might interest the reader to work a shift with us. I can lend you a pair of shorts, so come on; it's worth trying anything once. We have the morning watch, so after breakfast we have time for one quick cigarette before we change. 9.10 sees us walking over to the dining-room in shorts and singlet, with battledress on top so as not to give the sentry on the gate any cause for comment.

In the dining-room members of the team are assembling, together with Archie Cheyne, who is letting us down. As the Germans are still in the camp, we busy ourselves with the washing-up so as not to be thought loitering. If you look out of one window you will see the tennis-court makers starting work, while from the other you see an oldish man reading a book in a deckchair. He looks very innocent, doesn't he? Actually he is Captain Blackburn, R.N., our look-out. As soon as we are down he will come in and spend the morning on some innocuous-looking job over by that row of hat-pegs there, one of which, of course, operates the red light switch. Ah! he is taking off his spectacles and polishing them; that is the signal that the coast is clear for us to go down.

While we are taking off our jackets and trousers and stowing them in a locker, Archie Cheyne has the grating up and opens the trap-door. Quickly, and in the order in which we are going to start work, we drop through – it looks dark, I know, but it's only about three feet – first, Lieutenant-Commander Rupert Lonsdale, R.N., captain of the watch, then myself, then you, followed by 'Schoolie' Broad, 'Boy' Mewes, and 'Tich' Callaghan.

As soon as we are in we duck forward and start crawling along to make room for the others. Half-way down there is a joist with the electric light switch on it. My object is to get past this before anyone says 'Lights,' because in the prevailing damp it can give one a nasty shock. 'Lights working O.K.?' says Archie Cheyne. Thank goodness, there it is, just above your head, not mine. The light goes on to reveal quite a sizeable boarded-in chamber, flanked on either side by a brick wall. At the trap-door end is a pit, in which is put the day's earth. Next to it comes a tree-stump, which is the carpenter's bench. Beside it is stacked a pile of bed-boards to be used as revetments. At the far end, to which we have now crawled, there is the shaft and, above it, the red warning light in a bottle.

With three hours down here we take it in turn to work at the face. First, Rupert Lonsdale, you, and myself go down. Tying handkerchiefs round our heads, we drop down the shaft. At the bottom we duck into the tunnel and make our way along it. It is circular and about two feet in diameter, so if you are reasonably short in the thigh you can crawl, otherwise you must worm your way along on your elbows. Every two feet the section of the tunnel is squared to allow the revets to be fitted. Down the centre of the tunnel runs a board to enable the bags to slide freely. It is hard on the knees, so one endeavours to plant them on the verge either side. I advise you to keep as far to the right as you can, because the electric light leads are to the left. Many a worker has got a nasty shock in his backside before now. A terrific thudding starts overhead, to be answered by one in my heart. It is only the tennis-court makers, but the tunnel is driven through sand, and I am always terrified of a fall. Probably a few bits of sand will peel off and fall down your neck as you go by, but one gets used to that.

After eighty feet we come to the half-way house. Here the roof goes up to three feet six inches to enable the hauler to sit upright. There is also a light, an air-hole which comes to the surface, between the two wire fences, and paper and pencil for communicating with the shaft. To give you a chance to get used to this strange world you had better start at No. 3. Whispering to tell you to send a note back for a top, bottom, and two side boards, Lonsdale and I continue down the tunnel, which branches off here at an angle of forty degrees, to make for some bushes.

By your side you will find a hook, so attaching the note to it you give a couple of jerks and it is rapidly hauled out of sight. Holding a rope in each hand you wait. The jerks come almost simultaneously to say that the boards are ready and that I have a full bag waiting to be hauled back. You take the bag first. No. 4, thinking you are asleep and have missed his signal, gives another angry jerk. The end, which you are sitting on, is pulled away and disappears down the dark passage. Cursing, you duck down to look for it, and after a short grovel around, during which you grasp the light wire and get a shock, you retrieve it and haul away. If you are not careful you will get the two ropes tangled up, but ultimately the bags are switched over and you send the full one back and the boards to the face.

Soon you get the routine going smoothly. In the next three-quarters of an hour you send about ten full bags back and the same number of empties to the face. At the end of that time we come back and join you for a change of positions. After a couple of minutes' deep breathing at the air-hole, you come up to No.

2 behind me. As we go down to the face the colour of the sand changes from yellow to brownish ochre and the air gets noticeably fouler. Lonsdale has just finished putting in a board, so at least you get off to a fair start.

Frankly, I loathe being No. 1. *You* have that mundane object, someone's backside, and a pair of shoes just in front of you. For *me* there is sand ahead, sand all round. I am claustrophobic, and a quite unreasonable sense of panic clutches me every time I go there. For a quarter of an hour I dig ahead almost savagely to prohibit thought. Scooping the sand back between my legs like a dog, you cannot hope to keep up with me, and the pile of earth grows.

As soon as I have gained two feet I look round to ask you for the revets. Seeing the mound of earth behind me, half-way up to the roof, I panic again. My head is beginning to ache and I see circles in front of my eyes. Protesting that I must have a breather, I worm my way back over the heap and lie down, keeping my nose low, where there seems to be more air. You are delighted to have a rest and do likewise. After a couple of minutes I go forward again with the boards. Now is your chance. I am rather clumsy, and it will probably take me half an hour to get the top revet fitted. You ought by that time to be well through with that accumulation of soil. Holding the bag between your knees, you fill it with long scoops of the palm. With an effort, in the limited space, you turn it over, find the hook, put it on, and jerk. Away it goes, while you regain your breath seeing the rope runs out smoothly. Hauling the empty one back with one arm while you rest on the other one is also a difficult movement.

Meanwhile I am having trouble with my revetting. A shallow trench has been scooped out and the bottom board laid in position. A similar one has to be made above for the top, but at sufficient height to slide the side supports in. It is a tricky operation, and I am just beginning to feel too ill to go on when the light flicks twice. Hurray! our spell is over, and without further ado we crawl back.

It is pleasant to take a couple of deep breaths at the air-hole as we pass, but there is no time to waste. It is difficult at first to stand upright in the shaft after spending so long bent double, but soon we are up in the gallery. As No. 4, who does the long haul back, is the hardest job of the lot, we take it in turns to pull five each, and the man at the top of the shaft keeps tally so that we can judge what progress the watch has made.

Lonsdale is going to do No. 4 first, so I can show you what to do at No. 6. In the sand-pen there are about forty sausage-shaped affairs, made out of German face-towels, sewn up double. These have to be filled with sand (but not too full, mind you), so that the sand can be taken out of the dining-room. You'll learn soon enough exactly how it is done.

No. 5 is the easy job – nothing to do but hoist one bag up the shaft every few minutes and tick it off on the tally. Optimistically I start to clean myself up, brushing sand from my hair, ears, knees, nose, and shorts. Five bags up. My turn to go down the shaft and yours to take No. 5. A sharp jerk on the rope and I begin to haul. There is so much stretch in the rope that it takes four long pulls to get the bag moving at all. After that I know exactly what will happen. At seventeen it will slide into view and at the twenty-fourth pull it will come to hand. You drop the empty bag down to me – a shower of dry sand follows it into my hair – I hook on and away it goes. As usual, to clean up has been in vain, and I am covered in wet sand from coiling the rope in my lap.

I hear a soft 'ssh' above me, look up, and see the red light is on. Lonsdale switches off the lighting, to warn those at the face, and replaces the ventilation brick in the dummy wall. 'What is it?' you ask. 'Probably Herner, the oily, fat Feldwebel, going into the galley to scrounge a cup of tea,' I reply. No, it isn't, though. Through the wall can be heard voices. It is the ferrets carrying out a routine search . . . deadly silence . . . why is it I always have an irresistible urge to cough on these occasions? . . . that's them going away, thank God.

Soon the red light goes off and we resume work. You're in luck, though. Probably that quarter of an hour has saved you from having to do any hauling.

Sure enough, just as we are about to change places, there is a bang on the floor, and Archie Cheyne's voice comes through, 'Below there, get ready to come up.' Two flicks of the lights passes the news on. We start to clean ourselves in earnest. I should shake out your shoes if I were you; we don't want to take too much sand into the dining-hall. The other three arrive back, looking distinctly 'headachy'. Schoolie says they got another revet in, but that there is quite an accumulation of sand to send back.

We hear the grating being removed, and up comes the trap. 'Hurry up there, the mess caterers will be along any minute.' Standing up to give ourselves a final shake, we jump out. Arthur Green, the tunnel carpenter, is waiting to go down over lunch to put in another six-foot section of floor boarding; also Roddy, to lengthen the flex. Without further ado we put on our trousers and coats. It is good to light up a cigarette and get into real fresh air. Rupert Lonsdale comes up to us and says, 'Will you two get the bags up at lunch? I'll watch out and Schoolie will be in the cabin.'

Walking across to the showers I explain to you the drill. Every lunch-time, while the Germans are out of the camp, yesterday's B.B.C. news is read out. This is brought to us from an outside source, and we employ the time while it is being read in getting up the bags. Schoolie will go over and sit in the Commander's cabin, the near end of No. 3 barrack. If any German seems likely to come into the camp, Schoolie opens the window. The dining-room look-out can see this, so that the news stops and the trap is closed.

A cold shower dispels the worst of our headaches, and we are just in time for lunch. As soon as we have finished our bowls of soup we see George Elder, Camp Signals Officer, getting up with the news in his hand. He raps for silence. That is our signal, the trap-door is opened, and we pass up thirty-five full bags. They are stacked under a table, with coats draped casually over it.

While we are eating our bread and cheese a curious scene is being enacted at the door. Each member of the tunnel scheme, as he leaves the dining-room, goes and bends over the table, at the same throwing his jacket over his head. Beatty and Archie Cheyne then throw one of these bags over his back, and his jacket is lowered over it. Holding it carefully in position, the luckless victim is allowed to stand up. He is then pummelled and beaten till the sand has been moulded to his shape and he can do up the strap of his battledress. Looking as nonchalant as he can, he disappears in the direction of the garden.

As soon as we have drunk our mugs of tea we, too, submit to

this indignity, and then stroll innocently over to see how our tomatoes are doing. Soil disposal is the chief problem of any tunnel. There may be anything between thirty and forty tons of stuff to be got rid of, and it is not the colour of the topsoil. Our principle is to scatter a little here and a little there. You can, if you like, empty your bag in the static water pond, or down the main drain, or sprinkle it evenly over the garden paths, but over there amidst the tomatoes stands Lieutenant Van Kyrke, R.N., our disposal king. He takes a great interest in ullage pits. A base of sand, covered with tea leaves and potato peelings may not make the finest garden manure, but it does get rid of a lot of embarrassing soil.

We stroll past him, letting our bags drop as we go. Our job has now ended, so what better pastime is there than an hour's sleep in the sun? If you were thinking of watching Arsenal v. Chelsea this afternoon, I'll see you on the ground immediately after appel.

For nine weeks the work on the tunnel went steadily ahead. So did the internal preparations within the camp. Every evening, when the Germans had gone out, the classrooms became mapping rooms, with people busy tracing their routes from the original maps, which had been, for the most part, stolen from visiting lorries. There were escapers' German lessons, most realistically run – usually in the form of charades. To people proposing to travel by train, the teacher would appear as a member of the Gestapo and ask them where they were going and why. The potential hikers would be assured that they were in a forest, and were then waylaid by a 'State forester'. These lessons did much to give confidence. They were run by Lieutenant Frank Jackson, a Special Branch R.N.V.R. interpreter, who will figure much in this tale later on. Speaking perfect German, good French and Spanish, as well as fluent Russian, he possessed an inventive and ingenious turn of mind which was quite invaluable in devising character parts and stories for escapers and in framing letters of introduction.

As the day approached, we introduced a system of night watches to gain all possible information on the habits and movements of the guards. Finally, a draw was held to decide the order in which we were to go out. Thirty-seven were scheduled to go, and I was to be the twenty-third.

But a short time after the draw the Germans began to show disquieting signs of suspicion. Throughout one morning they prodded all along the north wire with metal spikes. The tunnel was far too deep for us to worry much about this, but we were alarmed when surveyors planted a lot of red-and-white poles outside the wire.

The next move was the arrival of a band of Negro prisoners from Milag, to dig a trench eighteen feet wide and of the same depth round the outside of the camp. This would prove fatal to our efforts, but we only needed another week to complete the job. So, to gain time, the S.B.O. told the workers that such digging was illegal, being of a military nature. They loyally downed tools.

This must have confirmed the Germans' suspicions, and their response was immediate. Next morning at appel it was announced that our camp and the ratings would be changed over. We were to be ready for the move by two o'clock. That afternoon a motley collection of farmers' carts, station barrows, and other conveyances arrived. Moving seven hundred people, together with their beds, cases, cupboards, mess-traps, supplies, and room fittings proved no mean task, but by the evening we were safely installed and so cut off from the scene of our past activities.

Ten days later the arrival, post-haste in the middle of the morning, of the Kommandant, Security Officer, and several other important people proved that the tunnel had been unearthed. They were, of course, delighted, and soon after it had been filled in we were moved back again to our side of the camp.

Total German victory was only averted by a fine escape made while we were still in the ratings' camp by Lieutenants Johnny Pryor, R.N., and Johnny Wells, R.N.V.R. Workmen putting up a new hut at the far end of the compound were able to enter and leave on production of special pink passes. One of them was a Belgian, and he loaned us his pass for a forenoon. It was promptly copied, and, dressed in workmen's clothes, Pryor and Wells succeeded in walking past the sentry at the gate during the lunch hour.

I had a grandstand view of this effort. The sentry at the gate was an old trading contact of mine, so I was detailed off to occupy his mind by engaging him in conversation. It was not hard to get him talking, but almost impossible to keep a straight face as these two familiar workmen shambled up. The sentry only glanced cursorily as they produced their passes, said 'Ja, 's gut,' and off they went down the road.

They were, unfortunately, the victims of the worst possible luck, in that their departure coincided with the first cold snap of the autumn. During the night they managed to get about ten miles distant from the camp. Throughout the next day, which was freezing cold, they lay up in a wood. In the evening, just as they were about to move off, the air-raid sirens went, which meant that the Landwache – German Home Guard – would be out. Theoretically, of course, they should have stayed put, but escaping is a matter of weighing one risk against another, and in their frozen state they reckoned it essential to move on. The result was that they stumbled into a patrol and were caught – an example of how bad luck can ruin even the best of escapes.

CHAPTER FIVE

AN IDEA STILL-BORN

SHORTLY after we returned to our own side of the camp, I devised a good plan. I had long felt that there must be some perfect and foolproof way of getting out of the camp. One day I hit on it.

There was a certain fairly standard form of document used by the O.K.W. (German High Command) for transferring prisoners from one camp to another. We had at various times seen these letters, and, as far as we could tell, action was taken on them without further ado. My idea was to get myself repatriated.

Lieutenant-Commander Linton, the camp paymaster, was going to get hold of some past letter, and with this as prototype I intended to have a letter written saying: 'At the request of the Foreign Office (Western European Section) Lieutenant James is to be repatriated. He will be escorted forthwith to Hendaye and handed over to the requisite Spanish authorities for transmission to Gibraltar. Inform the Kriegsministerium in writing what action has been taken and the estimated time of arrival of the prisoner at Hendaye.'

From the camp to Paris would have taken twenty-four hours. From there I proposed to wire some Spanish friends, and forty-eight hours after leaving Bremen I would be over the frontier. I reckoned that the Kommandant's acknowledgment to Berlin would probably take quite. as long as this to reach its destination. There would certainly be a further day's delay while the various office files were searched before anyone realized that it was a fraud. If they did realize what had happened before I was over the frontier, I still had the whole journey back in which to jump off the train, while if they bowled the letter out on receipt I could not be blamed, since a friendly guard was going to post it in an official envelope in the Wilhelmstrasse while on leave!

I still think it was the perfect scheme – to be escorted to freedom by one's captors and to have civilians cleared out of the trains to give one a seat. And it is wonderful to think what recriminations and dismissals there would have been when they discovered that I had been sent home on a fake! The whole of the War Office staff and clerks would have been suspect, and they could never have cleared up the mystery.

It is one of my great regrets that I did not have this idea sooner, but, as ill-luck would have it, they changed the German writer staff that same week and the new ones were not so corruptible. It therefore became impossible to get hold of the original, necessary for turning out a satisfactory forgery, and thus my flash of inspiration proved abortive.

There was at about this time a particularly fine attempt made; and one, moreover, that played an integral part in my own subsequent efforts. To relate it, however, I shall have to go back a bit. There was in my mess an R.N.V.R. lieutenant called David Jolly, who before the war had been in the C.I.D. From meeting him my opinion of Scotland Yard has risen even higher, for he was a most astute fellow. On first acquaintance he seemed a little dense, but behind an exterior of sleepy indifference he missed just about nothing.

In May the Germans had started a 'rest' camp in Berlin. What precisely the idea of this was we never discovered, but they took a house in a suburb of Berlin and to it sent about thirty officers from camps all over Germany. During their stay those sent were not the objects of any special propaganda, though they were from time to time visited by members of the Foreign Office. They were taken on sight-seeing tours two or three times a week.

Four officers from Marlag were sent there, and one of them was David Jolly, who had his plans already made for an escape. As he spoke very little German, the invaluable Jackson provided him with papers suggesting that he was Patrick O'Leary, an Irish stud-groom. As Ireland was the only part of the English-speaking world not at war with Germany, this was an excellent choice.

The problem of taking these papers with him to Berlin, when he was certain to be searched at both ends, was solved with great ingenuity. He had a wooden 'ditty-box', divided into two by a partition ostensibly to keep a ship's model in one half from being damaged. This partition, which was, like the rest of the box, of half-inch wood, was kept in place by four nails. Anyone could see that this was the case, since it was quite firm and the nail-heads were plainly visible from the outside. In point of fact, the two lower nails were fakes and the bottom of the partition was kept steady by an ingenious locking device. When this was undone it swivelled up on the upper nails, revealing that the model was on a false bottom. In this space he was able to keep maps, papers, and money that ultimately survived two or three police searches.

After they had spent a few weeks in the rest camp David Jolly and the three others were sent to a camp just outside Berlin because of air raids. It does not seem to have been very well guarded, for after a few days he escaped by climbing a tree. For two nights he walked due north and then caught a train to Stettin on the Baltic coast. Finding nothing there, he went on to Lübeck. Again he drew blank, so he continued by train to Flensburg on the Danish frontier. It was while trying to cross this on his sixth night at large that he ran into a frontier patrol and was recaptured.

During his absence the rest of the party were brought back to Marlag. Jolly rejoined us in the last week of September, just as my Spanish scheme was falling through. Besides bringing back sketch plans of two sea ports and several photographs, his effort was most valuable in the lessons to be learned from it. The two main points of interest to me were the ease with which a foreigner could travel by train in Germany and the lack of guards in the Baltic ports.

There was one fly in the ointment. The Germans were evidently beginning to clamp down on escaping. The maximum sentence under International Law for escapers was thirty days. To discourage us yet further, they court martialled David for 'uttering forged documents' and sentenced him to six weeks' imprisonment. As he had appealed, he had yet to serve his sentence when he returned to us, but it was a straw showing the way the German mind was beginning to work.

CHAPTER SIX

FIRST ATTEMPT—LIEUTENANT I. BAGEROV

OCTOBER came and went. I was well inured to the comfort-able round of camp existence, and it came as a severe shock one day to realize that with all my talk of escape and interest in it I had been in the camp nearly eight months without ever having had a run for my money.

There was an event late in the month which accentuated this feeling. About a hundred and fifty officers arrived up from Italy. The influx of new faces acted as a tonic to us. Many of them had made attempts to escape on the way, and for days we were entertained by their tales and experiences from the out-side world.

It was in the middle of November that I had my next idea, and it came by sheer chance. We were taken up every Thursday under guard to have a hot shower at a bath-house outside the main wire of the camp. This bath-house, as can be seen from the plan (p. 61), consisted of a long central shower-room flanked on either side by narrow changing-rooms, connected to it by open doorways. There was also a porch leading into the two changing-rooms.

As nothing untoward had ever happened on this bath party, the Germans had become very slack, and, instead of patrolling round the outside perimeter fence, they used to come inside to the changing-rooms and sit there smoking and gossiping until we were dressed and ready to move off again.

It was my invariable habit to have rather a quick bath as there were hot pipes in the bathroom on which I liked to dry my towel. These pipes were just by the frosted-glass window at the far end of the room. One day, while collecting my towel, I suddenly felt hot and opened one of the windows. At once I saw the blind spot in the German defences that I had been looking

60

THE BATH-HOUSE

MARLAG UND MILAG NORD

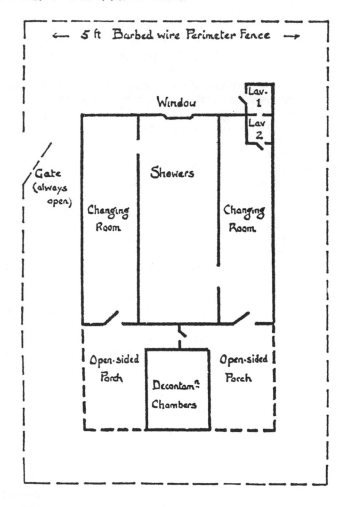

5 ft Barbed wire Perimeter Fence

Window

Lav. 1

Lav 2

Gate (always open)

Showers

Changing Room

Changing Room

Open-sided Porch

Decontam? Chambers

Open-sided Porch

for. As long as the guards were inside the changing-rooms, there was nothing to prevent anyone from dropping out of this window and just walking away....

As soon as I got back to the camp I registered my idea with Commander Beale. As he pointed out, there was only one snag to it, and that was how to manipulate the numbers; for the Feldwebel counted us carefully at the main gate before we left, the guards counted us again at the bath-house before marching us back, and the Feldwebel counted us yet a third time before sending us into our own compound.

This was a formidable problem, since unless the enemy could be fooled, I should have only half an hour's start, which in broad daylight was not sufficient. For several days we played about with ideas for two short men going pick-a-back in one large greatcoat, but were forced to admit that this was not practicable.

I decided, however, that the scheme was still tenable. I had two psychological lines of defence left. The first depended on the fact that whereas the prisoners stood only to get ten days cells for an escape attempt, the guards responsible got six weeks. Was it not reasonable to assume, therefore, that if they discovered that they were one short at the end of the bath, the guards themselves, who were actuated by fear, not patriotism, would rush the party through the gate in order to cover up their mistake and try and 'pass the buck' on to the subsequent watch?

The second consideration was that the Kommandant was hardly likely to inform all the local police that there was a prisoner at large until he had assured himself that the guards had not miscounted the original number of bathers. This he would do by holding a 'tally' appel. As I have related each man on his arrival in the camp was given a tally or metal disc on which was printed his number and the name of the camp. At a tally appel each man's name was called out, whereupon he came up and showed his disc while the Feldwebel checked the number against the official list. The weakness of this procedure lay in the fact that they checked bits of tin and not faces; for usually they did not glance at the man at all, but only at his tally.

It was essential for me to take my tally outside with me, since it would be my only proof of identity in the event of recapture, but I could leave a duplicate in the camp, and this I resolved to do. The dentist made me a spare one, cutting out the figures with his drill, and I arranged with a friend, similar in build, to act for me as well as for himself, if the need should arise.

I was also anxious to be covered for the afternoon and evening appels, to enable me to get well out of the district before the balloon went up. This was a much simpler proposition, because the Germans counted the sick in their barracks, and it would be easy, by having people in bed in about four different rooms, to induce the Germans to count the same man twice.

My method of departure was now organized, and I was reasonably assured of a twenty-four hour start. On the question of a route, David Jolly's experience had convinced me that the Baltic ports offered one of the best ways out of the country as the quays were not very well guarded and it should be possible to stow away in a ship bound for Sweden. Also profiting by his experience, I decided to go by train.

I even went beyond this. It was regarded as a cardinal rule of escape technique that one should walk to a station some miles distant from the camp before attempting to board a train. Since I wanted to use my twenty-four hours' start to the best advantage, and since most previous escapers had been caught while still in the area – remember the Kommandant's triumphant dictum about no one getting away from his camp, it was *too* close to England – I decided to catch the small gauge railway from Tarmstedt into Bremen.

On the face of it, this was absurd: to go to a station two miles from a prison camp in broad daylight and in halting German to buy a ticket. It was asking to be picked up. And yet was it? At mid-day there would be a strong presumption against any prisoner being at large without the alarm having been given. Furthermore, the very improbability of a prisoner doing anything so foolish itself lent the situation further security.

Escape is primarily a psychological problem. My ultimate success was due to the recognition of these two cardinal facts – first, that the guards themselves would provide the best cover for my escape; and second, that the shopping train would be perfectly safe. On these two tenuous links my chain of escape was forged.

When it came to a character part for my journey, I naturally

63

consulted the ingenious Jackson. He made the good point that the best possible guise in which to tour seaports was that of a seaman. As I possessed a naval uniform, this was easy. He suggested that I go as a Bulgarian naval officer, since Bulgaria was a monarchy, which would account for the Royal Crown on my buttons, and their Navy had only about three ships anyway, so I was unlikely to meet anyone who would know how they really dressed.

His final inspiration lay in the choice of my name. It was highly important that this should be easy to remember, because in the event of cross-examination it is the one thing over which one cannot afford to falter. Under the eagle eye of a Gestapo official it would be easy to forget a name like Vladimir Solokov, or Serge Filov. I therefore became Lieutenant Ivan Bagerov of the Royal Bulgarian Navy. (You may pronounce my name as you please. It is properly said like a well-known 'term of endearment used among sailors'. I ought to know; after all, there are none like it in the Sofia Telephone Directory!)

This choice of character touches on another most important point of escape technique – it was essential to choose an *unusual* type. Any German official worth his pay would know the proper papers for their own civilians, French 'forced' workmen, and others that they saw every day. But a Bulgarian naval officer or an Irish groom would only come their way at most once or twice a year, so any papers, provided they were sufficiently imposing, would suffice.

Mine consisted of a Bulgarian naval identity card and an open letter of introduction. The former was an approximate copy of our own naval cards. For a photograph we used the picture of a German E-boat hero, cut out of an illustrated paper. He did not look much like me, but it is a curious commentary on the gullibility of human nature that provided there is a photo and it has a stamp on it, it is most rare for the police or customs of any country to look and see whether it resembles the bearer. In any case to minimize this risk we put much of the stamp over the face.

There is a great art in writing bogus letters of introduction. They must be concise, yet contain a complete story, to save the escaper from answering too many questions. They must be vague enough to cover a wide range of possible activity, and they must be imposing without committing themselves to anything definite. In short, they must closely resemble answers to Parliamentary questions.

Jackson composed me a masterpiece. It said: 'Lieutenant Bagerov is engaged in liaison duties of a technical nature which involve him in much travel. Since he speaks very little German, the usual benevolent assistance of all German officials is confidently solicited on his behalf.'

Besides an official Bulgarian stamp – invented in the camp because we had no idea what the real one looked like – this letter was endorsed by three German stamps. One simply stated 'Heartily approved', and was counter-signed by some mythical official of the German Foreign Office. Another, apparently from the Chief of Staff at Wilhelmshaven, said: 'Permission to enter dock installations Nos. 9, 10, 11, 12, and 13 from 1st to 8th December.' This was so that as soon as I arrived in Bremen I could imply that I had just come from the west and not from the east. The third read, 'Identity checked by telephone from Berlin', and was signed by the Chief of Police at Cologne, whose name we had found in a German daily paper. This was to suggest that I had once previously been falsely arrested and had been released as soon as they discovered the mistake.

Most of the hard work for an escape lies in the preparations. Mine took almost three weeks and were very complete, for I was determined to enter as thoroughly into the character as I could. Bulgarians cannot pronounce the 'eu' sound in words like *Deutsch.* Instead of saying it like the 'oy' in boy, they pronounce it like the 'ye' in bye. To acquire this habit I used to read out aloud the leaders from the *D.A.Z.* and *Das Reich im bulgerien.* The Bulgar also uses Russian characters in writing, so in order to be able to make a signature similar to that on my identity card I had to spend ten minutes every day practising it.

I resolved to take a small case with food and a change of clothing. Every article of wear was marked with my new name, and I scraped the name of the maker off my soap and put a Bulgarian hieroglyphic on instead. There were two Greek officers in the camp, and, as the nearest possible thing, I asked them for their tailors' tabs and sewed them in my uniform and cap. By the time I had finished there was nothing on my person or in my case to suggest that I was English. I even carried in my pocket a series of 'love letters' written in off-Russian by Jackson in a very feminine hand.

It is most desirable to have something about one to distract the attention of any searcher from his job. I had the perfect thing to hand. One of my interests has always been the ballet, and when I was captured a friend very kindly sent me out some very fine half-plate photographs of the Sadlers Wells. One of these was a lovely full-face portrait of Margot Fonteyn in ballroom dress, from the ballet *Apparitions*. With her dark colouring and exotic beauty, this was just what I wanted. A short inscription in Russian was added, and she became my fiancée 'at the German Legation ball in Sofia'. The only time my case was ever searched, this picture occasioned far more interest than all the rest of the contents put together.

A number of articles I sewed into my clothing. There was a pocket in my trouser-leg in which I carried a recent letter from home to prove my identity to any neutrals or other potential helpers. My tally was sewn under one armpit and a spare sum of money under the other.

The only alteration or, rather, addition to my uniform was a five-letter flash – gold on a blue ground – on my left shoulder, standing for the initial letters of '*Kralov Bulgrski Voyenno-Mrskoi Flot*', or Royal Bulgarian Navy.

And now, just when I thought I had everything prepared, I found a weakness in my scheme. One day a group of prisoners were taken by train into Bremen to see the oculist. This meant that my uniform would be recognized on the local line. I was therefore forced to adopt an entirely different character-part for the first part of the journey.

I decided that I would travel into Bremen as a Danish electrician. My story would be that my nerves had been severely shattered in a recent raid, I had been spending a week in the country to recuperate, and was on my way back for medical survey. For papers I had a temporary identity card (*Vorläufige Ausweis*) and a note from the hospital (written, in fact, by Johnny Pryor) telling me to report there p.m. 8th December.

For my quick change at the bath-house I meant to go up in uniform with a greatcoat on, and with grey flannel trousers over

66

my blues, but rolled up above the knee so that they shouldn't show. I had a check scarf well tucked down underneath my coat collar and a cloth cap made out of a blanket, in one pocket. My shoulder-straps and belt were on hooks, so that they were readily detachable. The front buttons of my coat I covered with black silk, so that at a casual glance they looked like civilian buttons. To change then, all I had to do was to rip off the belt and shoulder straps, roll down my trousers, pull up my scarf, and don the cap. I practised this operation a number of times, till ultimately it took me less than thirty seconds.

All was now set. My final plan was to go up to the bath party, change, and drop out of the window, then walk down the road for about half a mile to where there was a small coppice. Here I proposed to kill half an hour putting on a few bandages and otherwise altering my appearance before walking to the station just in time to catch the 11.50 train. This train was scheduled to arrive at Bremen at 1.20 p.m. and start on its return journey ten minutes later. There would be such a crowd on arrival that I hoped to pass unobserved into the station lavatory. There I would discard my civilian clothes, and, once the train had left, emerge on to an empty platform as a Bulgarian. From then on my journey up to the Baltic ports should be fairly easy.

So many times had I rehearsed this scheme in my mind that I could almost believe I had done it. Only the play *Ten Minute Alibi*, performed in the camp a short time before, depressed me. For that showed only too well what a discrepancy there can be between the well-oiled plan of the imagination and its counterpart of obstinate fact.

The strange thing is that this one did run almost perfectly to schedule.

Thursday, 8th December, dawned cold and foggy. I awoke early and went to Mass; for I wanted to start with the blessing of God. After breakfast there was the usual last-minute rush to complete the preparations. The night before, I was sure that all was ready, but a whole series of last-minute details cropped up.

I had a small team of assistants for the job. There were Jackson and Bill Tillie to keep the guards talking and to per-suade them that nobody was away should they find their error. Johnny Pryor, the barrack escape representative, and Roddy were to come as close support. Their job was to stand in the doorways leading in from the two changing-rooms and to start taking their greatcoats off as soon as the guards entered. This would act as a signal to let me know there were no guards left outside the building, and prevent them from seeing me as I got through the window.

But long before we started out there was plenty for them to do. It must have taken six men to get me dressed and ready. Where was I going to keep my Bulgarian papers while posing as a Dane? It would never do to get them muddled up. Somebody suggested strapping them to the inside of my thigh, and rushed off to the sick-bay for sticking-plaster. I had better take needles and thread, but at the last minute could not find my 'hussif' . . . and so on. But at last my bag was packed. It had proved rather a squash getting all my food in, and my naval cap had to be jammed on top at the last moment.

The first bath party came back and reported that the guards were being slacker than usual. The second party were now up having their shower, so just before 10.45 we began to form up in threes at the main gate. With Jackson and Johnny Pryor, I was in the second row. Roddy, who was looking more villainous than ever and throughly enjoying himself, had volunteered to carry up my case and was a few rows farther back.

As the second party came into view, streaming out from the bath-house, I was seized with a spasm of acute regret. The day was grim and misty, and there was a nice fire burning in our room. I was happy and busy in the camp. Why was I such a fool as to leave when the war was bound to end in a few months anyway? Why risk being shot for a hundred-to-one chance of freedom?

The second party came through the gate and I got a thumbs-up from Commander Beale, who had gone to see for himself how the guards were behaving. There was a horrid feeling in the pit of my stomach when we began to move forward. I was committed now, and there was no way out, but how I wished that the Kommandant would cancel the last bath, or the water run cold, or something occur to get me out of this foolish venture!

I heard laughter behind me and the column came to a halt. Looking back, I saw Roddy, surrounded by three guards, stooping down. Hell! the lock on the case had burst and my gear was spread all over the road. I could see a packet of sandwiches sitting disconsolately by the edge of a puddle. How could even German guards fail to regard this as an unusual aid to bathing? But Roddy stuffed everything back again and closed the case, just as though he always took chocolate and cheese to his bath.

We moved off again, this time everyone straggling according to plan, so as to increase the delay in getting into the changing-rooms to give me more time to change. Roddy sidled up alongside and whispered to me that in repacking my case he had put my cap in the other way round. The badge now faced the hinge and not the outside. I thanked him perfunctorily. I did not then know that had it not been for this, I would certainly never have got away....

As I went into the changing-room I was already rolling down my trousers. Thirty seconds later I was a civilian and passed through into the bathroom. Roddy was standing by the far bathroom door. As soon as he started to take his coat off, I knew that the guards were inside. Looking round, I found that Johnny Pryor was doing the same. With a quite unnecessary clatter, which would have given the game away to anyone less sleepy than our guards, I climbed through the window and dropped out. As I walked past the bath-house I heard the sound of footsteps running on the concrete. Was it one of the guards? Was he going to shoot? I didn't dare look back, but continued to shuffle off as speedily as was consistent with innocence. Behind me I heard a door slam, and then all was quiet....

At once a new danger loomed ahead. Up the hill from the camp there was coming Joseph, a German who knew me better than anyone. He was riding a bicycle, his head lowered, after the manner of one pedalling up an incline. I had to turn right to gain the main road, but Joseph and I were almost equidistant from the turning. Could I get there first, and would he or would he not look up and spot me? I could not afford to run, but I reached the turn with Joseph still ten feet away. He never gave me a glance.

Despite fog and drizzle, the main road, which was absolutely straight and without cover for over a mile, was unduly populous. Two Germans I knew by sight passed me without giving signs of recognition. There was, in any case, nothing I could do about it except to trudge on, looking as innocent as I could. Apart from the worry, I was beginning to enjoy myself. All the anticipations and regrets vanished the moment I dropped out of the window and saw freedom stretching ahead down that long road.

I was in this happy frame of mind when a tall figure in field-grey, passing on a bicycle, gave me a dirty look and called on my to stop.

This first investigation was a great test, and I could hardly control my nerves.

'Who are you?'

'Paul Hanson – a Dane.'

'Where are your papers?'

'Here,' said I, giving him my temporary pass, which was imitation typewritten, in pencil.

'Where were you born?'

'Aarhus.' (Thank goodness I'd memorized all my details.)

'When were you born?'

'5th October.' (My mother's birthday.)

'It that your photograph?' said he, pointing at the small picture of a fair-haired man in golfing jacket, stuck on my pass.

With a nasty feeling in the pit of my stomach, I realized that I had grown a moustache, but had failed to add one to this photograph. Furthermore, he wore spectacles, and I had forgotten to take mine with me. Ignoring those discrepancies, I said, 'Of course,' in as pained a tone as I could. To my surprise he handed me back my pass without further comment.

'What are you doing here?'

'I am an employee of A.E.G., Bremen. I was wounded in the raid on the 23rd November and have been sent out for a week to rest my nerves. I'm now returning to the hospital for survey.' (This nerve story might discount any suspicion caused by my ill-concealed agitation.)

'Where have you been staying?'

'With the parson at Kirchtimke.' (There ought to be one at a place with a name like that.)

'Which one? What was he called?'

'I don't know his name. Everyone called him *"Pfarrer"* (*"Padre"*). The chap with the grey hair, I mean.' (A fairly good bet that there wouldn't be any young ones left.)

'H'm. Where did he live?'

'In the little house by the church.' (That is the usual North German lay-out.)

'Let's see inside that case of yours.'

Now I was for it. Propping it on the seat of his bike, I opened the wretched thing up.

'H'm. Shirt, bread, cigarettes, jersey. What's in that paper parcel there?' (pointing to my chocolate wrapped in an old *D.A.Z.*).

'More bread.'

'What's this?' (lifting the back of my cap. Thank goodness Roddy had turned it round.)

'My working cap.'

There was an ugly pause. He clearly had a residue of doubt lingering in his mind, which can hardly be wondered at, since he was the local policeman and we were still within half a mile of the camp. If he took me into custody I should be finished, for I could hardly survive a more searching cross-examination.

I produced the trump card, Johnny Pryor's letter, purporting to be from the medical superintendent at Bremen Hospital, directing me to report back that afternoon.

I gave it to him and the scales tipped in my favour. Pointing down, he said, 'Some of your cigarettes have fallen on the ground,' mounted his bicycle and was off. I stood in the middle of the road with my mouth open, clutching my case in both arms like a baby.

Continuing along along the road, I dived into a wood, bandaged my head, and shaved off half my eyebrows. The fog was thicker, and I emerged on to the road again just behind a girl carrying a small suitcase. Evidently she was catching the train too, so I followed her to the station. It was later than I had thought, and we had to run the last few hundred yards.

Buying the ticket presented no difficulty, and I climbed into a non-smoker full of typical German *hausfraus*. No one paid attention to the sad-looking young man with a bandaged head, who sat by himself in a corner. The fat woman opposite was soon fast asleep. It was just as well. Half-way to Bremen I looked down and saw that the silk cover had fallen off one of my buttons. Nobody appeared to have noticed, so I hid it under my cap and then cut it off.

It was 1.15 when we arrived in Bremen, and there was a crowd on the platform waiting to go back to Tarmstedt on the 1.30 train. Together with several others, I went into the public lavatory. It was primitive and the light was shocking, but there was a bolt on the door. With great excitement, for the situation was becoming increasingly Edgar-Wallace-like, I removed my civilian trousers and stuffed the cap behind some pipes. Off with button covers and on with the greatcoat belt. I then blacked my moustache and darkened my eyes, as I had been taught by the theatrical make-up experts. Finally, with buttons uncovered, Bulgarian papers substituted for Danish in my wallet, and my cap, complete with badge, set at what I hoped was a suitably rakish Slav angle, I stepped out on to an empty and deserted platform.

From my journey to the camp nine months earlier I remembered my way to the main station. Arrived there, I was faced by a fresh problem. There were two entrances, civilian and military. Which should I use, and ought I to buy my ticket before or after entering? Eventually I decided to try the military way in, but was stopped at the barrier and asked for my papers and ticket. I played dumb – in the American sense – and merely handed in my letter of introduction, saying 'Nicht Deutsch.' The R.T.O. read it through, nodding his head and saying 'Ja' to himself. Finally, he decided that 'benevolent assistance' was indicated, and a minion was sent to help me. This worthy escorted me along to the booking-office, bought me a third-class ticket to Lübeck, found out the time and platform of departure of my train, and finally took me to the waiting-room and ordered me a beer!

I was so bewildered by these developments that it took me some time to calm down. I could not but be most encouraged. Evidently my papers were going to see me through most difficulties, while my uniform appeared to be causing no comment. As a final test, I went up to a German sailor at the next table and asked him for the loan of a knife. He handed it to me without a word, and, German fashion, I brought a loaf of bread out of my case and cut off a large hunk.

Escaping is rather like that embarrassing social situation, when you meet someone who evidently knows you well but whom you cannot place. Luckily, having a shocking memory for names and faces, I have had plenty of practice at pretending to know and then asking innocent leading questions, such as 'How long would it be since we last met?' until I get a clue. Travelling through a strange country – and I had never been to Germany before – is like this on a vast scale. Without ever appearing ignorant, I had to learn the currency, what was and what wasn't rationed, whether one tipped the waiter, and lots of other points. Having so far paid for everything with a ten-mark note, I took my change along to the 'Gentlemen's' to see what the various coins were. Here another question arose. Should I put a penny in the slot or give it to the attendant? Eventually I did the latter, and spent the next half-hour learning which coin was which.

I caught the 4.17 train to Hamburg and arrived there without incident just after 6 p.m. Again ignorance led me into trouble. As one of the great junctions of the country and the main artery across the Elbe, Hamburg Station had some very sharp-eyed police about. It would have been possible for me to go from the Bremen to the Lübeck platform without going through a barrier at all, but not knowing the station lay-out, I left the platform at the wrong end and had to pass through three control points. One of these was a wicked place – a constriction in a passage, painted white and lighted by arc-lights, in which stood three Gestapo officials scrutinizing everyone who passed. I felt a lot better when I was through; for the fact that I was not stopped meant that I must have fitted in pretty well with my surroundings.

The waiting-room was packed, chiefly with soldiers on leave. I really felt quite sorry hanging my dear old naval cap up beside the Nazi ones with their high, stiff brims. It was like leaving a friend alone among thieves.

One could at that time still get a coupon-free dish in all German restaurants at lunch and dinner-time. This dish, called the 'stamm', was usually only a bowl of vegetable soup, but for a few days I thought it should be sufficient to keep my stomach full.

Sitting at the next table to me as I ate was a young soldier with an Afrika Korps flash on his shoulder. I suspect that he had seen R.N.V.R. uniforms before, for he kept on looking at me very strangely. I returned his gaze, and he evidently lacked the courage of his convictions, for he never came up to me.

When I left to catch my 8 p.m. train for Lübeck, I was stopped at the barrier and asked for my papers. The man just looked at my identity card, said 'S'gut', and let me go on. It struck me as rather amusing that he should accept without question a document in Bulgarian lettering. Only the serial number and the photograph were intelligible to a Western European, and the latter bore very little resemblance to me.

In the compartment of the Lübeck train, which was without light, a soldier and a civilian sat discussing the bombing. I was surprised at the open way they spoke, with a uniformed stranger in their midst, and soon after we pulled out of Hamburg they asked for my views of the situation. I explained that as a Bulgarian only recently arrived in the country, I hardly felt entitled to an opinion, and then took the opportunity to ask where there was a good place in Lübeck to sleep; for I was due to arrive just before midnight and did not fancy spending the night in the open.

They explained with emphasis that it was not safe to spend the night in any large German town in case of air raids. Was I due to go any farther? Yes, I intended going to Stettin the following day. Without giving me a chance to explain that I had business in Lübeck first, the civilian said that he, too, was going to Stettin, and that he would show me a very nice station waiting-room where he himself intended spending the night. Further, at the next stop he would see the guard and buy me a supplementary ticket. Feeling it better to let sleeping dogs lie than to embark on long and tedious explanations, I agreed to this.

We duly passed Lübeck, and an hour later arrived at Bad Kleinen, the junction stop for Wismar. Here my friend bade me get out and led me to what was a reasonably comfortable waiting-room, full of sleeping travellers. We found a vacant bench and sat down, but for me it was not to sleep. It had been an extraordinary day. Fourteen hours previously I had been in the camp; now I was the best part of two hundred miles away and on a coast full of promise. If I played my cards properly I should be home in a few weeks! . . . or possibly even days. . . .

At about 6 a.m. the next day I caught a train on to Stettin. It was fearfully crowded and ran very late. My compartment was full of soldiers of the young Nazi breed – swaggering and making far too much noise. At 9 a.m. there was a long halt just outside a place called Pasewalk. The carriage was getting stifling, but I looked at my watch with a certain sly satisfaction. Any minute now Tubby would be walking complacently to appel and the Feldwebel would go up and salute smartly and say: 'Ein Mann weg' ...

It was after 1 p.m. when we finally reached Stettin and I was beginning to feel very hungry, but with only three hours of daylight left there was no time to waste, so I set off in search of ships. Stettin must be by far the ugliest of all the Baltic ports, but it was exciting to be there, and for a seaman it was enough just to be beside a river again, with tugs and ferry-boats bustling about. Moreover, I was convinced that at any moment I was going to find a Swedish ship that would take me to freedom.

A couple of hours' walking speedily changed this view. I could find no free harbour, as I had supposed, and what ships I could see were Germans and in inaccessible positions. Actually I know now that my search was incomplete. To find the docks in a large town without the aid of some map or plan is no easy task. I naturally searched the main river banks from the west (or railway station) side; I did not know that I had crossed the main bridge I should have found extensive free quays a couple of miles to the eastward, connecting with the main river further down-stream.

As it grew dusk, therefore, my spirits fell and I became convinced that Stettin was no use. David Jolly – the only man I knew who had been there before – had drawn blank and so had I. The one redeeming feature was that I had walked round the harbour for five hours without anyone commenting on my uniform. I became yet more confident in the disguise even though I despaired of finding a ship.

To cheer myself up, I went on a combined stamm and pub crawl. At each of six water-front pubs I had a bowl of soup and a couple of half litres of beer, at the same time keeping my ears open for any sound of Scandinavian sailors.

A strange thing about some of these cafés was the little placard hung up in the bar saying, 'Wir grussen hier mit Heil Hitler.' Fancy an English pub having to display a notice saying

'The motto of this house is God save the King'! In any case I took the hint and thoroughly enjoyed clicking my heels and saying Heil Hitler with arm raised in every establishment I entered. By the time I reached the station I was taking a much brighter view of life, and even thought, as I had ample funds, of taking a train to Switzerland for a spot of skiing.

Finally, I resolved to try one more Baltic port, and took a second-class ticket to Lübeck. As the scheme of sleeping in a midway waiting-room had worked so well the previous night, I decided to try it again, and chose a place called Neu-Brandenburg, well known as a prison camp in the war of 1914–1918. On alighting, I mingled with a crowd of naval ratings and made for the waiting-room. We were just trying to open the door when an R.T.O. came up and told us that there was better accommodation going for Servicemen in the Wehrmachtsunterkunft (the German equivalent of our Y.M.C.A. station canteens), and ushered us firmly along there.

The place was certainly pleasant enough. A buxom Red Cross sister gave us soup and coffee free; there was a fire and a number of comfortable chairs in which to sleep. But it was no place for a British naval officer. There was a German N.O. sitting at the next table, and with him were about a dozen ratings. It was all very well to get away with it in the street, but sitting opposite them all night was a very different matter. Still, I could not very well leave, so I had perforce to continue playing my part. As soon as one of them started to doze off I began to nod. Of course, any idea of sleep was out of the question, but it was the most convincing part to play. . . . Crash! . . . what was that? . . . I looked at my watch. It was six o'clock and the last rating was going through the door. What extraordinary things occur! Entirely against my wishes I had spent a night in full uniform alongside an officer of the Kreigsmarine, and in official military accommodation too, and nobody had recognized me!

A few minutes later I was in the train rattling on towards Lübeck. By this time I was beginning to take rail travel for granted, but this was the one journey that caused me some embarrassment. A garrulous old man was sitting opposite, and he kept on quoting what sounded like proverbs or clichés at me in Low German. I could not understand a word he said, so merrily smiled and answered Ja' or 'Nein' as seemed best. Then I got up and gave my seat to an old lady. No sooner had I done so than I realized that it was not 'the thing to do'. People looked at me as though I were some creature from a strange world observing different customs. To make matters worse, I was jammed up against some little Hitler Jugends. I was always terrified of children. They are so quick-witted and observant. The ordinary man is not usually 'up' in types of aircraft, enemy uniforms, and the like, but it is just the sort of information on which little boys thrive. These lads only came up to my chest; I was frightened lest they should see the London stamp on the inner side of my Service buttons.

But the time passed, and shortly after 11 a.m. we arrived at Lübeck. My first need was for a shave, so by way of an experiment I went into a barber's shop and asked for one. It was an almost fatal blunder; for, as far as I could understand him the man told me that with soap rationing there had been no shaves for about two years, and who was I to know so little about things anyway. Muttering 'Ach so,' I left hurriedly, followed by many a curious glance.

It is a strange fact that although all my time at large in Germany was during good weather, in retrospect it seems as though the sun never shone. Everything there was so dull and cheerless, I can only visualize it beneath skies of grey. Other escapers have returned with exactly the same impression.

Lübeck was the only exception. A charming little town, it seemed a sort of backwater from the main-stream of war – there was more in the shops, the people seemed better dressed and more cheerful, and – yes, the sun shone. Just over the bridge was a comfortable hotel, and to this I went for my shave. The porter's desk was empty, so I locked myself in a bathroom, had a good wash, and put on a clean shirt and collar. I felt much better after that, and went down to the restaurant for lunch.

This meal was notable for the well-dressed people there – one couple in particular could have been transported straight to the Berkeley – and also for a two-course stamm, the only one I have ever heard of – a bowl of consommé, followed by a dry vegetable hash. This was the one trace of civilization I saw in the whole of Germany, and it made me long all the more for home.

Leaving my suitcase at the hotel, I started off on a reconnaissance in high hopes. If the geography of Stettin was hard, that of Lübeck was very easy, for here the river was flanked on either side by quays and warehouses, and these were the docks. Rather than walk down the verge between the warehouses and the ships, where I might conceivably have got picked up for taking too great an interest in the goings-on, I decided to use the road outside, which was full of trucks, dockers, horses and carts, and cover the opposite bank by peering through the occasional gaps between the warehouses. Taking the east bank first, I walked about two miles and, to my great excitement, saw two Swedish ships. That meant that they were still trading to Germany and were not shut in by Baltic ice, as I was beginning to fear. On the other hand, they were not of much use to me, since they were both auxiliary schooners, with decks piled high with lumber, so that, quite apart from the lack of good hiding room there is in a sailing ship, they might be several days yet in discharging their cargoes.

Just as the town and docks began to melt into open country, I saw far ahead of me a sight that made my heart jump – the masts and yards of a full-rigged ship.

The fast disappearing square-rigger has always exerted a great fascination for me, and in 1937–1938 – between leaving Eton and going up to Balliol – I had been lucky enough to serve a year in *Viking*, a Finnish four-masted barque, taking part in the so-called 'grain race' from Australia. The knowledge of the Swedish and Finnish languages and of the mentality of the Finns thus acquired was to stand me in good stead at a later date, but for the minute I decided to give escaping a rest and have a look at this ship

I went as close as I dared – to within about a hundred yards of her, perhaps – and she was a fine sight, with double t'gallant and royal yards gleaming newly painted in the sun; a shark's fin nailed to her bow-sprit end. A couple of boys were aloft tarring down her shrouds, and I recognized her as the German training ship *Schulschiff Deutschland*. As often before, it struck me as a great pity that Britain, a country dependent on her seamen, should be the only power to abandon sail-training. I am aware that there is no rational – that is to say, economic – argument why boys who are going to be concerned with ocean liners should learn the ways of the sailing ship. But the case is the same as that for a classical education. Why teach Latin to a future banker or statesman? The answer surely is that it gives him certain qualities of mind which will be of great value to him in after-life.

This argument applies to the sailing ship. I am actually writing this chapter* in a large liner. At the next table to me sit two apprentices – nice boys, with hair well brushed and buttons polished, in as natty uniforms as ever left Austin Reed's. A few minutes ago the steward went up to them with a menu and asked if they would like haddock, kipper, or bacon and eggs.

Will they make as good seamen as the old captain at the far end of my table, who spent five years as an apprentice in sail, and who, if he wanted any breakfast, probably had to put on his oilskins and make his way through seas waist-high down to the galley and fetch it for himself?

Will they, when they are sixty, have those mental qualities of resource and character which enabled him to get his ship through to Russia in 1942 on a Murmansk convoy, spending weeks in the ice in 79° 48° north, with 175 survivors of sunken ships aboard?

Are they, moreover, satisfying that innate love of adventure which sent them off to sea, or will they, in five years' time, feel frustrated and take some nice cushy job ashore, thus further reducing Britain's sea prestige and efficiency?

Such thoughts occurred to me as I gazed at the full-rigged ship, but soon I returned to reality, for one cannot afford to day-dream long on the escape trail. Retracing my steps, therefore, to the main bridge over the river, I started to walk down the west bank, looking east.

Almost at once I saw just what I was after – two coasters lying alongside, bow to stern, with Swedish flags painted on their topsides. For the first quarter-mile below the bridge the river was divided into two by a long, narrow spit or peninsula

* This book was originally drafted from my lecture notes in December 1944 *en route* for the Antarctic, where I spent 18 months surveying as a final naval appointment. – Author.

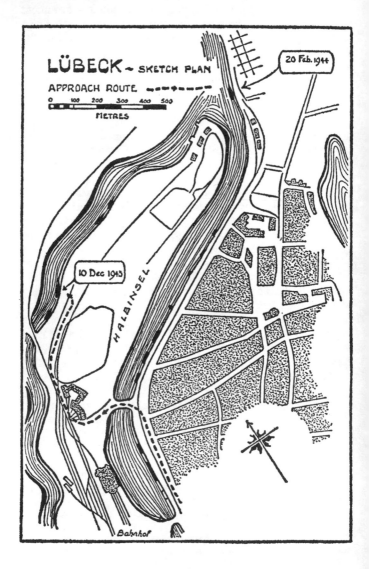

LÜBECK ~ SKETCH PLAN

APPROACH ROUTE ━ ━ ━ ━ ━ ━

0 100 200 300 400 500
METRES

20 Feb. 1944

10 Dec 1943

HALBINSEL

Bahnhof

80

called the Halbinsel, and it was alongside this that they lay. (See sketch plan, facing.)

Without further ado I turned for the hotel to get my bag. Since it was thirty-one hours since I had last been challenged, and as a bold and forward policy had always worked hitherto, I resolved to try to walk aboard in broad daylight, trusting that an authoritative bearing and decisive manner would prevent anyone from asking me my business.

It was after three o'clock when I left the hotel, and I was glad that things were going to be put to the test. I was beginning to feel the lack of food and sleep; also, one operates the whole time under certain nervous tension, and I wanted to get the matter settled one way or the other.

As I approached the Halbinsel I found that it was wired off with a gate and a sentry. This latter, however, had a beat nearly thirty yards long; for a road and a double railway track ran on to the peninsula through the gap he was guarding in the wire. Better still, there were some goods vans on one of the tracks, jutting out just beyond the line of his beat.

My line of approach lay along the main road and bridge, cutting across the Halbinsel, with the wire on my right hand. I adjusted my pace so that the sentry would have his back to me – i.e. be walking in the same direction as I by the time I reached the goods waggons. When he turned at the near end of his beat I was just walking down the road, apparently interested in a girl on the pavement opposite; twelve paces later and I dodged down the track behind the goods van.

I came on to the jetty, and there, ahead of me, lay the two Swedish ships. There were no sentries on the gangway, but I could not afford to hesitate. A quick glance – they both looked exactly the same – and I made for the nearer, which was loading coal. In a fever of excitement that can well be imagined I walked straight up the gang-plank. In front of me lay a companionway, so I went down it. Below, I found myself in an alley-way with doors on either side. I saw one marked 'Steward', knocked, and went straight in.

A pleasant, sandy-haired individual looked up as I entered. 'Excuse me, I'm an escaped British officer and I'm in need of help. . . .' A pause. . . . He got up, went over and locked the door.

So far so good. I began to have dreams of home by Christmas. He produced a cigar and a drink and asked me how I had got there. I gave him the outline of my story, and asked in return why he had demanded no proof of my identity.

'Oh, I recognized your uniform. I spent the first two years of the war trading on the English coast. You're R.N.V.R., aren't you?'

After three days of furtive wandering, with nobody to talk to, it was a relief to be able to gossip quite freely with this man! The precious minutes began to slip by. . . .

'And now to business, steward. I want to get to Sweden. Can you hide me away anywhere?'

'Sure. Just you wait here and I'll go and arrange it with the Chief Engineer.' A few minutes later he came back with a long face. 'It's no good. The Chief says that she is low on coal and due to bunker tomorrow. That means there will be stevedores crawling about the ship everywhere. Your best plan is to go to the ship astern. She's a motor-ship belonging to the same company, and she's due to sail today sometime. Her steward is a good fellow – took some Russians to Gothenburg last trip. Offer to make it worth his while and he'll certainly hide you away.'

I argued the point. I felt so secure aboard this ship that I was loth to leave her, even for a fifty-yard walk down the jetty, but at length the steward persuaded me it was the best thing to do.

I had to wait a minute at the bottom of the companionway while a bulky individual, evidently the skipper, came below. When I reached the deck they were casting off ropes on the jetty. As I watched, the gap between the other ship and the wall slowly grew. Was it worth making a dash for it? Obviously not. A pier-head jump would cause far too much attention. Even if there were no police or a pilot aboard, some bystander would certainly report the occurrence and she would be stopped farther down the ten-mile river. No, I had missed her, and that by seconds.

I returned to my steward friend, who went on deck to see for himself. When he came back he had already made up his mind. 'It is no use your staying here,' he said, 'you will be in greater danger than if you are ashore. Have you money?'

'Yes.'

'Well, stay away till Monday. If you come back, I'll take you to Gothenburg. Till then, the best of luck to you.'

A moment's thought. There was obviously some force to his arguments, and anyway I could not well run him into trouble. It had been quite easy getting into the dockyard area; it should be no harder to get out. Yes, I had better go. My hopes were still high as I left the ship. I had got my passage arranged. I could spend Sunday taking a trip up to Rostock for a look around in case there were anything better.

My return route was at right angles to the sentry's beat. I tried to time it to pass the danger zone when his back was turned, but I was just too late. As I walked away down the road a voice shouted after me 'Halt!' I turned, trying to look as innocent and indignant as I could.

'What were you doing in the dockyard?'

'Seeing off a friend; the mate of that ship that has just left.'

'Where are your papers and dockyard pass? What, you have no pass? Then you must come with me to the guardhouse.'

I was taken there, and an escort was provided to take me to Battalion Headquarters. The Duty Officer was impressed with my papers and with my protests at the indignity of arresting a distinguished allied officer. He explained to me that it was his duty to check up on me since I had no pass. Could he look in my case?

As there was nothing incriminating in it, I showed it to him readily enough. He went out for a few minutes and held a conversation next door. When he returned, it was to say that the Kommandant thought it would be best for me to go to the police station: 'just to get everything regulated'. It was a suggestion admitting of no refusal, and as my only possible line I agreed with outward enthusiasm, but with a sinking feeling within. My chances of fooling the professional police were slim – and the stories one heard of the German police were not encouraging. . . .

We arrived at a building on the water-front marked 'Wasserschutzpolizei'. They were, I suppose, the German equivalent of our Thames River police. Thank God it was not the Gestapo, anyway!

A fat, red-faced man listened while my escort told his tale; then, turning to me, he asked for my identity card. I gave it to him, and made a vigorous protest against being arrested. Paying no attention, he went over to a cupboard and took out a magnifying glass. After scrutinizing the card for a minute, he looked up and said: 'Where did you escape from?' The game was obviously up, but I said stiffly: 'I am afraid I don't know what you mean.' He replied: 'Yes, you know perfectly well.'

I gave him my full name, rank and camp, and produced my tally in support. His first action was to call in a junior, and together they congratulated the man who had arrested me. He was naturally delighted, and stood looking on with a grin from ear to ear. He, too, probably had visions of being home for Christmas.

The red-faced man showed the other my pass, and then, turning to me, said scornfully: 'How did you expect to leave Germany on a rotten pass like that?'

Before I could reply, the other cut in and said: 'Not at all. When you think of what few facilities they possess in those camps it's a very fine bit of work.' Turning to me, he pointed at the stamp of the Chief of Police, Cologne, and said: 'Look, that is your one bad mistake. You've put "Polizei Kommissar". It should be "Polizei Präsident".'

I was searched for weapons and asked to make a statement. I had no intention of playing around with the German police, so I made one, substantially true, but lying on all key points. They cannot have known anything about camp life, for they wrote down quite happily that I had walked out of the main gate at dusk when the sentry was not looking!

I had a strong desire – presumably a sort of defence mechanism – to boast of my time at large, and I derived the greatest pleasure from telling them of my night in the Wehrmachtsunterkunft at Neu-Brandenburg. The man with the red face grew yet redder, and there were broad grins on the faces of the rest. The news of my capture seemed to have spread, for quite a number of others had come in to see the specimen. Baiting Red-Face in front of such an appreciative audience was great fun. . . .

I was asked how I had got into the prohibited zone. Not without a certain feeling of satisfaction, I turned and pointed at my captor. 'Past him, when his back was turned.' Broad grin quickly vanished.

'At what time?'

'About 3.10.'

To the sentry: 'Were you on duty then?'

Sentry: 'Yes.'

One of the police went over to the telephone and rang up the C.O. I should not be the only man in jail over Christmas!

The questions being finished, the nasty one left the room. The younger man immediately offered me a cigarette, and I in return shared the rest of my chocolate with him.

A few minutes later he was detailed off to escort me to the local military jail. On the way there he informed me that the camp had been told of my recapture and would fetch me in a couple of days. He added as a rider to this that he was sorry, personally, that I had had such bad luck.

Taking advantage of his friendliness, I said: 'I suppose, of course, that you knew I was at large?'

'Naturally,' he said. 'We had a full description of you in the office yesterday.'

It was a lie. Why, I had to write my name out for them and spell the address of the camp. It would be useful for future reference to know that the Baltic ports were not informed when we were at large. I'd have to try that route again some time.

It was dark when we arrived at the military jail. Again I was searched, and my name and rank were put in a large register, but I was allowed to keep my small case and all my gear. A jailer led me along a dark passage till we came to a massive door. It was opened for me, and I entered a small cell. Behind me the door clanged, and, worn out, I fell on to the hard bed and went to sleep. . . .

CHAPTER SEVEN

BACK UNDER ESCORT

THE two days I spent in Lübeck jail were ones of acute misery. Curiously enough, the immediate reaction was one of relief – relief that the mental strain of the past three days was over. It was on awaking next day to my cup of ersatz coffee (for or instead of breakfast) that the full blast of icy disappointment hit me. With no way of foretelling the future, it seemed as though my only chance had gone. Throughout the long miles from the camp fortune had miraculously attended me. Every obstacle, every difficulty, had been overcome. More by good luck than anything else, the final cordon had been penetrated and I had been alongside a ship, cleared and ready to sail. Yet I had failed to board her.

Minutely and in every detail I went through the previous twenty-four hours. One mental picture in particular haunted me. When I had first seen the two ships from the far bank of the river, it had appeared that the bow of one overlapped the stern of the one ahead. In the excitement of seeing Swedish ships this had made no impression at the time. Yet should I have deduced from it that she had cast off her back-springs and was preparing to sail? Or mightn't it equally well have meant that she had just arrived? Had I in my excitement, when alongside the first ship, paid adequate attention to the second? No. Could I have told that she had steam up? As she was a motor-ship, no. How about my interview with the steward aboard the first ship? Had he indicated to me that there was any cause for haste in going to his friend aboard the other? Actually he had not. Had I spent too long arguing with him, cajoling him? The deletion of any single remark would have made the whole difference between success and failure. Were all my remarks really necessary? No, they were not, but how could I deduce the urgency of my cause? My reluctance to leave my haven of safety, once achieved, was understandable enough. Was it culpable? Backwards and forwards, up and down, I argued with myself, at one minute feeling that it was a clear dictate of Providence, at the next sick with remorse and regarding the failure as the outcome of my own stupidity. One thing alone was clear, and that was that the chance of a lifetime had been missed.

With such pleasant thoughts as sole companions I spent Sunday, 11th September, in my cell. I could just walk three full paces from one end to the other, and with arms outstretched I could touch both side-walls at finger-tip distance. I had only two visitors. One, the officer of the day, was a local schoolmaster. It was terrifying to think of such a man being in charge of youth. He was totally incapable of distinguishing between fact and opinion, and it was as impossible to argue with him as it is with one possessed by religious mania, for there was a fanatical gleam in his eye against which reason itself was powerless.

My other visitor was the rather amiable little corporal of the guard – by trade a shoemaker from Cologne. With him I did not attempt to talk politics. He was convinced that Germany was going to win the war, but nevertheless asked for a written testimonial in English and Russian to the effect that he had treated me well. He was unable to see any inconsistency in this.

On the following day – Monday – the corporal said that he had got me a specially good lunch – so good, in fact, that I would undoubtedly wish to stay there over Christmas. This *specialité de la maison* consisted of about a dozen potatoes boiled in their jackets, accompanied by sauerkraut and swimming in thick, oily gravy! The pathetic thing was that he genuinely did believe he was giving me an unusual treat.

I was sleeping off this princely repast when, at about 2 p.m., the door of the cell opened and two guards from the camp arrived to escort me back. One was Hermann, the chief 'ferret', a sly little Hamburger, who spoke very good English; his companion was a sleepy fellow, by profession a drummer in a Hamburg dance band. Hermann was abusive, called me a bloody fool, and ordered me to strip for searching. He went carefully through my clothes, but failed to find my little compass, which was hidden in the double lining of my fly-buttons.

After informing me that I was a desperate character and that he would certainly shoot if I attempted to escape on the way home, he led the way to the Hauptbahnhof. I was given no chance there. Indeed, it was not worth running much risk to get away; for I had no money to get to any other port, and it was only reasonable to assume that had I got clear, a very careful watch would have been kept on all Swedish ships in the neighbourhood.

We arrived at Hamburg about 6 p.m., just as the All Clear sirens were going after a heavy American daylight raid. As there was rumoured to be 'trouble on the line', my guards refused to go any farther and I was taken to the Militärunter-suchunsgefängnis – a mouthful that means Army Remand Cells. Here my shaving kit and tooth-brush were taken away from me – when I protested and demanded to see an officer, no notice was taken – and I was locked in a dark cell. On a wooden ledge I found two coarse blankets and promptly took refuge in the only haven of prisoners – sleep.

Sixteen hours later, having in the interval been brought neither food nor water, I was released and handed over to my guards. When we got back to the Hauptbahnhof we were told that the district line from Harburg to Willemsburg, the main artery from Hamburg to the west, was out of commission. At Harburg we detrained and queued at the main gate. Outside the station there was a large crowd trying to get lifts down to Willemsburg, and it was the evident intention of the authorities to prevent our trainload from adding to the crush.

For a quarter of an hour the passengers queued on the platform willingly enough. Then they began to get restless and bored; finally, they broke and ran across the line, down the embankment, straight over the stationmaster's cabbage patch, and so on to the main road. My two guards and I were in the van of this ugly rush. As we trampled down the vegetables I offered Hermann my parole – it was not going to be easy getting back to the camp, and it was as much in my interest to get home as theirs, for I had not fed for over a day and war-time travel was as tedious in Germany as anywhere else. My parole was accepted. I was first over the fence on to the main road, the guards passed over our cases and their rifles, which I held while they followed me.

Though it was nearly twenty-four hours since the raid had taken place, the Germans had made no effort to arrange an emergency bus service. In this respect their organization compared ill with ours. I remember being at Waterloo in the 1940 blitz, waiting to catch a train down to Southampton. Suddenly the line was hit just outside, and the station closed down. Within ten minutes a fleet of buses had arrived, all the pasengers were taken to Surbiton, and the trains started punctually from there. The Germans, on the other hand, left people to fend for themselves. Whenever an army lorry or other form of conveyance drew up it was stormed by an ugly crowd of ill-tempered people. Usually, strapping young soldiers, who could easily have walked, managed to elbow their way aboard, pushing out poor old women with their pathetic little bundles of salvaged belongings. They were left in tears by the roadside.

At this juncture Hermann proved himself a man of some push. He approached an officer, told him that he was guarding a 'particularly dangerous' escaper, and said that he must have transport. Accordingly we were given priority in the next car.

All the way to Willemsburg the road was littered with worn-out elderly people. Whenever I have seen any tendency in our Press to gloat over the destruction of Germany, I always remember that scene. At the very best, bombing is a ghastly necessity, and the aged and infirm refugee is as pathetic a figure in Germany as anywhere else. One woman, struggling along with a suitcase, tried to board our van at a cross-roads. The soldiers tried to push her off; such transport was not meant for civilians. She burst into tears, saying: 'Aber mein Mann ist auch Soldat,' and someone took pity on her and helped her in. She regarded this elementary act of courtesy as such a favour that she insisted on giving her helper a strip of coupons out of her ration book.

When we neared Willemsburg the cause of the trouble became apparent. An engine and several coaches were lying on their sides diagonally across the tracks, and for several hundred yards the place was littered with débris. The station was crowded and closed, but we managed to gain the platform by climbing down the girder support of an overhead bridge.

Even more wonderfully, we managed to get into a train going to Bremen, and the train ultimately left. As usual, the sleepy guard was soon snoring, but Hermann was enjoying himself. He obtained a good deal of reflected glory from detailing my escape, together with embellishments of his own, to our fellow travellers. Curiously enough, though they were all Hamburg refugees, they displayed no antipathy to me; in fact, one old man wished me better luck next time and offered me a sandwich. There were some schoolboys in the next compartment who overhead the conversation, and one of them came over to me and said: 'Please, meester, what is de time?' Curious people, the Germans.

Then just when I was beginning to feel that most of them were quite decent souls who had been cruelly misled, the old arrogance reasserted itself. I was asked why we had declared war on peaceful Germany. For the hundredth time I explained it was because of their attack on Poland.

'Ah, but that was different.'

'How about Holland, then?' I said.

'Holland,' came the reply, 'was always part of Germany. She spoke a Germanic language and was due to return to the Reich, anyway.'

I suggested mildly that that was hardly the view of the Dutch, but was told that they'd soon learn to see better sense. . . . Everyone agreed with the speaker, and thereafter political conversation languished.

The topic turned to air raids. As in England in 1940, every town had its champion and everyone in the carriage had had a narrower escape than anyone else. The whole of the old town of Kiel was said to be in flames; another man said that there was nothing left of Leipzig except craters; a third had been washed out of his home when the Möhne Dam was hit . . . and so on *ad nauseam*.

We reached Bremen a couple of hours late, leaving us only just time to catch the last train to Tarmstedt. We were seated, jolting down the little line, when the guard came in to collect tickets. On hearing that I was a prisoner he exploded. I thought he would rupture a blood vessel, he shouted so loudly at my escort. They both shouted back, and the rest of the carriage joined in. For a minute I was afraid that a lynching scene might develop, but luckily the argument got so fierce that its cause was forgotten. Finally, with civilians cursing the bloody Wehrmacht and my guards cursing the verdammt stay-at-homes, we removed ourselves to the van. The only regrettable part of this performance was that the ticket collector would probably recognize me if I were to travel again on that line.

It was 10 p.m. before we got back to the camp. I was taken up to the German guard-room and put in the cells. The corporal produced black bread and ersatz coffee – my first meal since leaving Lübeck thirty-two hours previously – and on that I went to bed. My first escape attempt was over.

CHAPTER EIGHT

CHRISTMAS INTERLUDE

I DISCOVERED that my guard was a most delightful German called Willi Fischer. He told me next morning that in peacetime he had led a Hamburg dance band and was well known to the English and American tourists. He asked anxiously about the latest damage to his home town. I told him, apologizing rather lamely for the necessity which had caused it.

'You needn't worry about that. *C'est la guerre*, and in two years' time, when your tourists start coming back again, it will all be forgotten.'

I take off my hat to anyone of any nationality who can take that view. If more Germans were like Willi Fischer, there would have been no war.

There was also an inmate of the next cell. He was one of the guard company who had been found in possession of over four thousand English cigarettes – trading profit. For this he had been given ten months' imprisonment by a court martial.

At 10 a.m. I was taken to see Lieutenant Schoof, the German Security Officer. His house in Bremen had been destroyed the day before and he looked years older. Although many disagreed with me, I liked him. An old Merchant Service man, he had been trained in sail and had served several years in the famous *Potosi*. He had then entered our Merchant Navy, and was Second Officer of a British ship when the war of 1914 broke out. He had therefore spent nearly five years in internment, during which time he had made several attempts to escape. It was only natural that he should have considerable insight into the prisoner mentality, and he had taken the trouble to send down to the camp for cigarettes and food for me. For nearly an hour we talked sailing ships, and then I was asked about my escape.

I had all along decided that the best thing to do would be to draw a red herring over my trail. The first step towards confusing him was to repudiate the copy of my 'confession' which the Lübeck police had sent to him, on the grounds that my German was not fluent enough to enable me to understand the questions put to me. The only two things that I wanted to keep secret were my method of exit (from the bath-house) and my using the local train into Bremen. There was no point in denying that I had travelled by train after that; for there was no other means by which I could have got so far in so short a time. I had taken the trouble to memorize a different series of train connections in order to falsify my time of departure, and these I gave with a wealth of petty detail to give an impression of frankness. When asked how I had got into Bremen so quickly, I said I had been given a lift by car. When asked what the car was like, I said it was dark so that I could not see. I then naïvely and virtuously said that I could not possibly say how I left the camp, leaving him only one false assumption to draw – that I had escaped from a medical party that went up to Milag for an X-ray the evening I left. If the guards on the bath party had already reported that they were one short that day, I would have run myself into a beautiful trap for perjury, but since there had been no search party at Tarmstedt or on the train, it seemed a fairly safe bet that my absence had not then been reported.

To my relief the story was accepted without comment, and that afternoon I was sent down to the camp cells. In the evening the Feldwebel of the watch – a nice fellow with whom I had done much trading – came in and upbraided me for getting him into trouble. He said that he was on duty the afternoon after I left and had not bothered to count the evening X-ray party when they returned. I felt a complete cad for getting him into quite unmerited trouble, but was relieved to have confirmation of the success of my plan. Later the Kommandant came in and said that I had been sentenced to ten days in the *bunker* (the delicious German word for punishment cells) for my attempted escape. I should also, in due course, be court-martialled, like David Jolly, for 'uttering forged Identity Papers'!

A quiet period in a little cell all to myself was rather a

pleasant change after living for nearly a year in a room with seven other people. I had my bedding and pictures brought over, and I was allowed my own food and as many books as I liked. For the first day I was kept rigidly apart from any contact with my friends in the camp, but this was soon unofficially relaxed, and I was able to make dates and talk to them through the lavatory window.

The Germans had just called up the 50–56 age group to guard prisoners, and it was quite interesting talking to these older men. Of ten with whom I talked, eight were violently opposed to the war and hated the very name of Hitler. It was significant, however, that while they would all grumble to me while they were alone, if there were two of them together they would shut up like clams.

One of them was particularly pathetic. A rather frail prematurely aged man of fifty-five, he had been captured by the British in 1916. During captivity he had been particularly well treated, and had, as a result, a great love of the British. His only son, of whom he was very proud, had recently returned from the Russian front blinded and minus an arm, so he had a deep and almost personal loathing of Hitler. He himself was so blind in the dark that whenever I wanted to go to the lavatory, which was about forty yards from the cells, I had to take him by the arm and lead him there so that he could be with me to guard me!

As a result of his bitterness against the régime he was most anxious to help me to escape. He knew Lübeck well and told me much about the shipping movements there. For example, he said that there was a forty-eight-hourly mail steamer from the SVEA Line wharf, opposite the police station where I was arrested, to Gothenburg.

A further advantage of the *bunker* at this time of year was that we were just passing through a particularly cold snap and, unlike the rest of the prisoners, I always had enough coal. There was a totally inadequate ration of fifteen coal briquettes a day in force at the time, but part of my 'punishment' was that I had to go up to the coal dump with a Red Cross box to draw my own ration, and as the guard changed at midday I used to draw it twice – before and after the change of guard! This gave me such a surplus that I was able to pass eight extra briquettes through the wash-place window each evening to one of my room-mates. At night I allowed the guard to sit in front of my fire instead of standing watch in the cold passage outside, but he had to pay for this favour by keeping it going and heating my morning shaving water.

The only fly in the ointment was that my sentence was not due to finish until Boxing Day, and I was very keen to be with the rest of the camp for my Christmas dinner. Actually the Germans did not behave too badly. I was allowed out for Midnight Mass on Christmas Eve, and again for morning Mass on Christmas Day. The Feldwebel of the guard could not free me in the evening, as the Kommandant had sent down special instructions to say I should not be released, but a couple of friends were allowed over to talk to me while I ate in my cell. The day was further enlightened by no less than six of the German guard bringing me in little presents – a nip of cognac, a few apples, or a bag of sweets. There are good, bad, and indifferent Germans like the rest of us – the only trouble is that instead of locking the bad ones up they put them in the jobs where they can do most harm.

I came out of the *bunker* on Boxing Day to find that Roddy had at last raised a party to cut through the barbed-wire behind the cells. It is a measure of how keen Roddy was, that it was less than a month since he had returned from having his appendix out in Milag. He is reputed to have come round from the anaesthetic asking what the chances were of getting out of the hospital!

Two pairs were going on this scheme. Roddy had as his mate a very nice fellow known as Mac, and the others were two recent arrivals up from Italy – Davies and Balkwell. These two had originally wished to try the scheme from the *bunker* itself. For days they hung about the main gate, with pipes in their mouths and hands in pockets, waiting for the German Kommandant to come into the camp so that they could fail to salute him. Finally he came, the studied insult was observed, and they were had up. After a severe talking-to the Kommandant let them off with a warning! The next week the little comedy was repeated, and this time they got four days' cells. After all that, their trouble was wasted, for it proved a quite impossible place to escape from.

Now Davies and Balkwell had joined up with Roddy and Mac and were scheduled to go by the wash-place roof as soon as the moon had waned sufficiently on 29th December. I was one of the support party, whose job it was to see that no German was inside while they climbed across it. This was a horrid job, waiting out there in the dark wondering if any sentry would spot them. For cold-blooded courage I think cutting a way through a barbed-wire entanglement within a few yards of men with loaded rifles takes a lot of beating. Finally, it was safe to assume that they were away, and we returned thankfully to our barracks.

We expected the alarm to go up long before 9 a.m. appel next day. Actually it did not, for the simple reason that the sentry who first saw the hole in the wire covered it up in case he were blamed for letting anyone get away. So appel saw us there in unusually good time. Normally there were not many takers for the front rank on parade. Pyjamas under trousers and great-coats were less conspicuous in the rear. This day was the exception. It was grand to be in the front row of the stalls and see the Feldwebel go up to Tubby to make his report. 'Vier Mann weg.' 'Was ist dass?' – seldom has the smile left anyone's face so quickly. . . .

It was not, unfortunately, long before we had more news about the four. Roddy and Mac walked the twenty-four miles into Bremen in about eight hours – a good show by the former for a man only just out of hospital – went to the main station and bought tickets for Rheine, fifteen miles from the Dutch border. They arrived there at about 3 p.m., and as there were plain-clothes men on the platform were forced to leave. They started to walk towards the frontier, looking for a wood so that they could lie up until dark. Alas! the fates were against them. They could find no cover, and the road was never deserted enough for them to leave it. About half an hour before dark they were overtaken by a policeman on a bicycle, and that was that.

Davies and Balkwell, being only just up from Italy, spoke no German, and had therefore decided to walk to Holland – a tough proposition in mid-winter. They were both finally caught after ten days at large – a fine performance in shocking weather.

Our other excitement at this time was the more homely one of a splendid Christmas pantomime. It was typical of the ingenuity of prisoners that our small community could produce such a show. In a camp containing three hundred and fifty in all, the pantomime had a cast of forty-eight and over sixty characters. Entirely written in the camp, it was a skit on the Navy, acted with immense gusto by the Navy. The lyrics were set to popular dance tunes.

The scheming villain, who was, of course, after the heroine, succeeded, during his middle watch, in getting two very drunken Marines to put the wardroom piano in the hero's cabin. The Marines were then put in cells. When the piano was discovered next day, what could be more natural than for the hero to be court-martialled 'for theft of piano, Admiralty pattern Mark II, one, officers, for the use of'?

The court-martial scene will long live in everyone's memory. One of the court arrived late in cocked hat and bathing trunks, explaining that as his boat had broken down he swam. Another was permanently asleep and had to have his cocked hat taken off by the President whenever the articles of war were being read. The President himself interrogated the accused as follows:

'Did you or did you not steal the piano?'

'No, sir.'

'Well, what the blazes are we here for, then?'

But best was the Paymaster Captain reading out, very fast, the articles of war to find out what constituted a 'ship' within the meaning of the act. For those who have designs on Admiralty pianos, it is as follows: 'A ship shall include any ship, vessel, boat, scow, dhow, yacht, bum-boat, barge boat, prison camp, etc. (applause) but shall not include an M.T.B., M.G.B., M.L., S.G.B., H.D.M.L., T.L.C., L.T.C., C.L.T., or any other Coastal Force or Combined Operation vessel.' (Cries of execration from all captured at St. Nazaire, and Dieppe.) The scene ended up with a rousing chorus, 'Who stole the wardroom piano and the piano's lid? Yes he did, no he didn't, yes he did, no he didn't, yes he did, no he didn't, YES HE DID,' a parody on a then popular dance tune. The prisoner was then dismissed from the Service.

Ten days later the villain was celebrating his engagement to the faithless girl, when Marine Blogg, just released from cells with a (happily) returned memory, entered and confessed all. At this point all ended happily, for the hero was reinstated and the villain disgraced.

The German censor had to see the dress rehearsal of this spirited show. He left shaking his head sadly, and gave it as his frank opinion that though he had never previously believed the propaganda about the degeneracy of the Royal Navy, what else could he assume of people who made fun of their own Service in such a fashion!

As a result of Roddy's wire-cutting venture the Germans imposed a curfew on the camp. We had to be in our barracks by dark and were not allowed to move about the compound. To see that we obeyed this order two men with well-trained and fierce-looking police dogs patrolled the grounds during the hours of darkness.

It was unfortunate that this curfew came into force on New Year's Eve, as elaborate plans had been made for a celebration, including beer and music in the theatre. It all had to be cancelled. The situation was further complicated because the Germans had been given an issue of wine and spirits by the Führer, and most of this had already found its way into our camp. I myself in an hour's trading bought seventeen bottles of champagne and six of schnapps. Naturally, by midnight most of us, unused as we were to alcohol, were fairly mellow, and at one minute it looked as though there might be an ugly scene, for hilarious prisoners do not worry about little things like bullets and dogs. Somebody was imprudent enough to kick one of the unfortunate animals, which (somewhat reasonably) bit him, and after that the party quietened down a little. The New Year was sung in traditionally with 'Auld Lang Syne' and 'God Save the King', and by one o'clock most of us were safely in bed.

After this I started again on preparations for escaping. It did not seem wise to make use of the bath-house again; for although the German officers had not discovered how I had left the camp, all the other ranks knew. This was for two reasons. First, the guards at the bath party had noticed that they were one short. After a hasty consultation they decided to push the party quickly through the main gate so that my absence should not be laid at their door. Secondly, a German called Charlie, the 'coal-führer', whose mission in life it was to see that we never drew more than double our fuel ration, was in the village shopping on the day in question, and came out of the local just in time to see me racing down the street to catch the 11.50. Not being on duty that day, he had not felt it to be any job of his to stop me, but he did mention to our orderlies on his return, 'Oh, by the way, I saw one of your officers on his way home this morning – he damned nearly missed his train, you know!'

Thus my method of departure was common knowledge to the German troops. They had therefore decided among themselves to take steps to stop any recurrence, and now patrolled outside the bath-house instead of coming in, as before. So it was obvious that it might take time for this method to become ripe again.

I had plenty of other irons in the fire, though. As a result of the five of us having all got well clear of the district in such a short period of time – the evident lifting of the camp hoodoo – interest in escaping had risen to a new pitch, and many schemes were under discussion.

Escaping is largely a matter of supply and demand. Nobody in his senses prefers going out of a camp as part of a mass break or by tunnel, as opposed to the single and well-covered departure. The snag of the latter is that there are comparatively few methods available, and once used they are unworkable until the guards get slack again. Thus, if more than a certain number of men intend to break out in the course of a year, some mass method must be devised.

Accordingly I turned my mind to this problem. From nine months' trading I knew the form of the guards pretty well, and there was one man I was certain would let me out for a sufficient consideration, for he had often sold me things of a blatantly contraband nature, such as wire-cutters and torches. On the theory that he might as well be shot for a sheep as for a lamb, I suggested that he let twenty-five of us out over the wire at two hundred cigarettes per head – five thousand in all – payment to be made after we left the camp.

He seemed quite willing to discuss details. It was only to the southward that there was no trench outside the wire, and we agreed that that would have to be the stretch used. When a particular guard company came on watch – every third day – they moved round one place clockwise, and as there were nine posts it would be twenty-seven days before he came to this stretch of wire. Luckily this would be all right as regards the moon, but he very sensibly insisted that there must be no snow on the ground for the tracks to give him away. On this plan, with the approval of the Escape Committee, we agreed.

It did not take long to raise the twenty-five volunteers, and soon everybody was hard at work preparing their kits and routes. Most favoured the Baltic ports, but there were several going west, one to Switzerland, and three to Denmark.

At this juncture the Germans sent another big draft off to the Channel ports, and one of them was my 'contact'. The setbacks of the escaper are many.

It was then decided to reopen Mabel. On the way back from Lübeck, Hermann, the chief ferret, had told me that the only reason why they had not discovered it sooner was because they did not realize that *they* had built two walls under the dining-room. Since they had left the second wall and simply filled the space between with earth, the obvious answer was to make a trap-door at the far end over the old shaft and sink it again. It would be surrounded on three sides by walls and on the fourth by earth piled up to the floor joists, and the last thing a German would think of would be for us to sink a tunnel in the same place as the one he had just discovered. Work was put in hand with this right away.

At the same time our invaluable Jackson came up with a brilliant scheme for a solo exit. Briefly, the idea was for him to be put over into the German compound on a dark night and to follow the change of guard out at 7 p.m. As a plan its very simplicity lent it perfection. For clothing he only needed the correct silhouette, since colour would make no difference in the dark. The British Army greatcoat would be good enough with belt and ammunition-pouches of wood tacked on, while a wooden rifle and a cardboard German helmet could be knocked up by the theatrical people in an evening. Even if by any chance he were to be addressed going through the gate, the odds were that his perfect German would enable him to get away with it.

Once outside, he intended to travel as a French veterinarian called François Lefoulon, and, with typical thoroughness, he spent weeks learning up his French and German veterinary terms and wandering round the camp asking the guards what they did with their cows when they had colic, in case he should be asked to do any veterinary work on his trip down to Switzerland.

The day before he left I was talking over his plan with him, and he said that he wished his papers had not all been made out or he would have changed his name. I asked why, and he told me that he had invented a visiting-card which would tip the wink to any Frenchman produced to verify his identity, but would be unlikely to be seen through by a German. It was as follows:

```
M.P.R. Fide Albion
            Aix-Chappé
```

There are some ingenious fellows in the world, and he was certainly one of them.

At the same time another part of four – Godfrey Place, of midget submarine fame; Frank Carr, of Coastal Forces; Bill Tillie, taken at St. Nazaire; and Brooks, an ex-Italian *prigioniero* – were anxious to cut through the wire at the same place that Roddy had used a month earlier. Their argument was that the Germans would least suspect a place only recently used, and, anyway, there was no other ... they were all unusually resolute men.

The main obstacle to Jackson's scheme was the dog-men. Luckily, ever since the New Year's Eve riots they had shown an increasing tendency to slacken off, and several of us were actively engaged in promoting this trend. At first, no one could leave his barracks at all after sunset. After a few days one could get permission to go from one hut to another. Later it had become customary merely to give them a hail and say where one was going to, and the idea was growing not to hail at all. They were, furthermore, very proud of their dogs and could be relied upon to give a demonstration of their prowess on request.

So if we wanted to do something illicit at one end of the camp it was only necessary to get some stooge to say to them, 'Is it true that if I run across the football field your dogs will knock me over?' and they were safely out of the way, for the next quarter of an hour!

On Wednesday, 2nd February, Jackson was ready, and as the night was dark early he was put over the wire by ladder into the German compound before the dog-men even came into the camp. This went very smoothly, for we had staged a dress rehearsal in the gym that afternoon. As soon as he was safely over, the ladder was taken to bits and hidden all round the camp. I was on duty at the main gate to intercept the dog-men with friendly talk, but was recalled – 'operation completed and ladder stowed' – before they arrived.

Jackson was due to buy his German gear, catch the last train into Bremen, and be beyond Hanover by morning appel on Thursday, 3rd. We then intended to blow his departure, lest in the afternoon they should blame it falsely on the bath party. We had not banked on German efficiency. A new prisoner arrived in the camp on Wednesday evening. They failed to add his name to the list, and therefore reported all present and correct on all Thursday apels!

On Thursday evening, which was not as dark as its predecessor, the wire-cutters were ready to go. Bill Tillie thought it was not dark enough – a decision throughly borne out by events – but the rest were determined to have a shot at it, since a raid warning had doused the perimeter lights and the moonless season was advanced.

Success attended them as far as the German compound, since the dog-men were inveigled into a room for a cup of tea. Suddenly a loud shout was heard from the main gate, and all the searchlights were focussed on the wire. Feeling rather sick, we waited for shots, but none came. A few minutes later a German came into the camp with instructions to transfer their bedding to the cells. . . . He said they were all right, but that the situation had been 'verdammt gefährlig' (damned dangerous).

Next day a note, brought back with their breakfast things, told us the tale. Reaching the outer wire, they had started to cut. Unfortunately the cutter had too soft an edge, grew blunt, and started making a noise like a pistol shot at each stroke.

Godfrey Place, undaunted by the experience at Alten Fjord which gained him his V.C., and by the eight weeks' solitary which followed it, relieved Frank Carr on the cutting. On the last strand the sentry heard, called out a warning, and covered them with his rifle as the lights went on. It must have been a shattering experience, but they kept their heads. Place and Brooks managed to throw their papers, already weighted against such a contingency, into the ratings' compound. Frank Carr jettisoned his in the guard-house fire.

The results of this gallant operation were not without fruit, for when the Kommandant boasted at appel on Friday morning that his vigilant guards had intercepted all three, he was told that, on the contrary, one, Jackson, had got away. Thus the best method of leaving the camp lived for use another day.

Before Jackson left, I had completed plans for my next attempt by my former method as it looked as though the Germans were already slackening off at the bath-house. I therefore had my letter of introduction drafted and translated by him into German officialese. I had decided this time to go as a Swedish Merchant Service officer, since a seaman's rig was calculated to cause no suspicion in the neighbourhood of the docks. During my time in the camp I had heard once or twice from an old Swedish friend of windjammer days. He had told me that he was mate of the s.s. *Adolph Bratt* of A/B Bratt, Gothenburg. I decided to use the name of this ship, so that a search of Lloyd's Register would show that my vessel existed, but lest I should compromise him, I chose another name and called myself Christof Lindholm.

My story was that while the ship was discharging cargo in Bremen I had been caught in the daylight raid of 24th December and had been badly burned. After two months in hospital I was being repatriated. Since I was anxious not to be recognized on the local train into Bremen, this story enabled me to assume a most effective disguise, worked out by the camp doctor in conjunction with a theatrical make-up expert. To simulate burns, the hair was shaved back off my left temple, half that eyebrow was burned off, and the whole side of my face painted with acriflavine to suggest newly healed tissue. A series of scabs was superimposed, made out of bits of cardboard dyed in Friar's Balsam and stuck on with glue. The whole was covered in a concoction of violin beeswax and surgical spirit. The result when dry was a horrid 'gooey' mess calculated to cause anyone to avert their gaze.

My letter was a typical Jackson product. Purporting to come from the Swedish Consul in Bremen, it said: 'Christof Lindholm, mate of s.s. *Adolph Bratt*, was badly burnt in the American terror raid on 24th December while his ship lay in Bremen. He is now on his way to rejoin her. Since this subject of a friendly Power has suffered so much both physically and mentally during his stay in Germany, it is trusted that the authorities will do everything in their power to make his journey home a pleasant one.'

We had a new forger from Italy – Lieutenant-Commander O'Sullivan, R.N., a Fleet Air Arm pilot. To the best of my knowledge his forgeries were responsible for getting five prisoners home during the war. Although keen on escape himself, he spent most of his time exercising his talent for others. It must have been a disheartening job; for probably not more than one in ten of his clients ever got home, and if they did, they naturally received the credit and applause. He not only forged the letterheading and stamp of my letter from the Swedish Consul, he also turned me out a most beautiful 'Temporary Swedish Passport'. This document was such a masterpiece that I was quite happy to go anywhere with it.

To save my showing these papers in the neighbourhood of the camp, I had a different set for use as far as Bremen. To cover my departure from the bath-house I was to be a surveyor looking at the drains. For this purpose an architect in the camp prepared me a plan of the bath-house drainage system, while Johnny Pryor made me a camp pass.

This pass was part of a strange coincidence. Johnny asked me what serial number over three hundred I would like to have on it – we knew that up to three hundred genuine ones had been issued, and it is just as well to be correct in every detail. For no very definite reason, except that I am rather fond of multiples of three, I chose 369. Although that particular pass was never used, the lucky number I had chosen did come up again at a very critical juncture. I am no believer in the superstitious at all, but I shall mention this in due course as an example of the strange way the escaper's mind is apt to work.

I decided to use my uniform again, but this time with Merchant Service buttons and cap badge. To give me a further line of defence and to obviate wearing nautical garb in the neighbourhood, where it would cause suspicion, I took with me a complete set of civilian buttons with metal rings sewn to the back. With the aid of split pins I could then change my greatcoat from Merchant Navy to civilian in a matter of seconds, while removal of the badge would do likewise for my cap. Again I took with me a small case containing toilet gear and food, and again all its contents were marked with my assumed name.

Everything was now ready and it only remained to find a suitable day. I had decided to go on the 12.15 bath party. This would mean missing the 11.50 train from Tarmstedt, but would allow more time for me to receive reports from earlier parties on the behaviour of the guards.

There was one other improvement on my former scheme. Attached to the changing-room was a lavatory outhouse with two compartments. (See plan, p. 61.) One led straight into the changing-room; the other was entered from outside by a door kept permanently locked. There was a wall between the two but it was just possible to squeeze over from one side to the other through a gap below the pent-house roof. I had learned to pick locks from our ex-C.I.D. man, David Jolly, and planned to adopt this method rather than use the bath-house window. The advantage was that I should have more time to change. For cover I still relied on the guards themselves not reporting my absence.

On three consecutive Thursdays I came to 'immediate notice' – that is to say, the patient doctor, Lieutenant-Commander Knight, R.C.N.V.R., applied my disguise, I packed my bag, and had my papers ready to be dated. (This latter could only be done when departure was fixed, or it would have entailed reforging them every week.) On each occasion, however, reports on the guards' behaviour were unfavourable, and the operation had to be cancelled.

CHAPTER NINE

FINAL ESCAPE

THURSDAY, 10th February, seemed propitious. It was snowing hard and the first bath party reported that the guards came in, instead of patrolling outside the bath-house.

Immediately I went to action stations, though it needed the usual four or five helpers to ensure that nothing was forgotten. At the last minute I had made a pair of Harris tweed leggings to cover my naval trousers during the first part of the journey. These, pressed by the Catholic priest, who possessed an iron, had to be pinned on to my ordinary trousers above the knee. Then my disguise was applied, papers dated, food collected, and my bag packed. I was just ready in time for a quick lunch, and then, asking the Mess caterer to retain my uneaten cheese against my return, and with a few hasty good-byes, I joined the bath party.

As before, Johnny Pryor came in support carrying my case. The snow gave me ample reason to hide my 'scars' with a balaclava over that side of my face. On the way up my spirits sank to zero as on the previous occasion. The moment when one exchanges a quiet, safe existence for one of unknown discomfort is always pretty grim. Added to that, I should have to lie up in a wood all day until dark, and such a prospect in deep snow was not enthralling.

At the bath-house, straight to the lavatory: quick assumption of disguise – off cap-badge, down leggings, and on with civilian buttons – Johnny gives the signal that all the guards are in the changing-rooms, and stealthily I pick the lock. The bent nail engages; one turn, a second turn – dash it, what a noise it makes! I should have had it oiled in advance – and then I am outside. The snow-squall providentially reaches its peak and nobody is about. . . .

Head well down, I walked up the road trying, while in sight of the camp, not to go too fast. A quarter of an hour brought me to the wood. It was hard to enter it without leaving tracks, but a piece of frozen ditch in the lee of a thick bramble provided the way. Stooping down, I tied my shoe-lace to see that the road was clear both ways. It was deserted, and in I went.

It was impossible not to leave tracks inside, but they would soon be obliterated and the snow would make it impossible for dogs to follow the scent. It took me some time to find good cover; ultimately I discovered the ideal, a small plantation of young firs about eight feet high and in rows three feet apart. Once within and I was invisible.

Comparative safety was my hide-out's sole merit. Snow fell on me with monotonous regularity and it was damned cold. My feet were soon numb and dead. It was not only literal cold feet I suffered from either. I soon began to curse myself for every sort of fool. Why had I left the warmth and safety of the camp on such a crazy venture? I was certain to be caught, in all probability on the road to Tarmstedt. It would be a sad contrast with my previous attempt, and I should have to go through all the weary procedure of the *bunker* again. It would be three weeks this time, and there was still the first court martial for forgery to come ... and probably a second.

In the distance I could hear the police-dogs baying. Had the guards reported my absence? Were they following me up? Horrid thought! I began wondering if I could possibly slip into the camp again unobserved. If I went back after dark I might be able to bribe a guard to let me in ... but how could I face my friends ...? No, I should have to play the foolish farce through to the bitter end. I had no one but myself to blame.

To retain the secrecy of the forged camp pass, I decided to adopt my Swedish story right away, and I buried the plan of the drains and the pass itself. It was better once I was doing something. So that I should not have all my teeth drawn in the event of recapture, I decided to distribute my money. As long as I could keep hold of a little it would be worth trying to make another break on the way back. Keeping thirty marks in my wallet, I put a spare ten in my trouser-leg pocket, which again carried a letter with an English stamp and postmark with which to prove my identity. I then sewed twenty marks into the lining of my greatcoat.

By this time it was beginning to grow dark. It had originally been my intention to leave at about 7 p.m. and go with care to Tarmstedt, getting off the road whenever I saw traffic. It was not till 7.30, though, that it was dark enough, and then I had to walk fast to catch the train at eight o'clock. That was the last train, and, as previously, I attached a very high importance to being well clear of the Bremen-Hamburg-Hanover triangle before the balloon went up.

When I stepped out on to the road I was aware that this was really the time of test. If anything had gone wrong with my cover in the camp I would run straight into a patrol at the station. Once safely in the train and I was more than half-way home. As I walked briskly down the road it stopped snowing. There was a good moon, and fair-weather clouds chased each other across a clear, frosty sky. A crash to my right put my heart in my mouth, but it was only a stag, which bounded swiftly over the road. I thought of the stags on the hill at home in Scotland and it struck me as a good omen. To be active and free meant a good deal, and I suddenly felt that even if a patrol at Tarmstedt awaited me, three weeks' cells was little to pay for such a walk over the heath.

A soldier on a bicycle passed without comment – a good sign. I met several pedestrians, who paid me no attention. It looked as though all might yet be well. The train was not in when I arrived at the station, but the Kommandant's car was there and several soldiers. Was this a patrol? There were some goods trucks on a siding lying in shadow, and, while waiting, I ducked underneath. As this would be hard to explain away if I was spotted, I laid my wallet on the line so that I could say that I had dropped it and was searching for it. A few civilians and a soldier came and stood by my truck. They were only a few feet away, but as long as I stayed still there was little chance of being seen.

Eventually the train came fussing in. A reconnaissance of the booking-office revealed no troops, so I joined in the queue. At the window I proffered a ten-mark note for a ticket costing 1m. 30. The man told me angrily that he had no small change. This was a bad mistake, but I had nothing smaller on me, and I slipped into an empty carriage. At length the train pulled out. Luckily the ticket collector who came for my ticket was not the one that had caused the row a month previously, but he was very suspicious when I explained that I had no ticket through lack of small change. He flashed his torch in my face and scrutinized me carefully. In view of the fact that I was manifestly foreign, that there was current an epidemic of escaping of which he must have heard, and that it is unusual for travellers to have no small change, it was astonishing that he did not ask me for my identity papers.

At the next station I was able to get my ticket, sold to me by a soldier on leave, and thereafter the journey to Bremen was uneventful. I took a tram to the Hauptbahnhof, and arrived just after the last train to Hamburg had left.

As the next slow train did not leave till 4.25 a.m., I decided to spend the night in the waiting-room. The station police were inspecting papers, but I was keen to give my pass a trial run, and the danger was less than the wastage in strength and morale involved in passing such a night in the open. It proved to be a model inspection. I pretended to be asleep when the man came up. He looked at my passport and asked if I had any other papers. I gave him my letter, which he read through, nodding and saying 'Ja' to himself. Finally he folded it, gave it back to me, and said, 'Thank you very much, that is all in order. Good night.' – What an escaper owes to the 'back-room boys'!

Soon afterwards the air-raid sirens went, and I was forced to go down to the shelters. It was the nastiest night I have ever had; for the R.A.F. were continually droning overhead, and the prospect of a 'block buster' on the station did not appeal to me one little bit. The Germans in the shelter seemed no more enthusiastic than I, and showed a strange mixture of apprehension and apathy. I noticed with interest that there were private rooms off the public deep-shelter, with visiting-cards pinned on the doors. I managed to take a peep inside one, to find that it was quite nicely furnished. Evidently leading citizens were able to hire them for the duration – a curious proceeding for a 'National Socialist' country. My chief terror was of being unmasked, for an ugly scene might have ensued. People kept on brushing past me, and I was afraid lest they should part my overcoat and see the blanket-stitch tops and safety-pins of my tweed 'trousers'.

It was 4 a.m. when the All Clear went. Having passed the station police examination, I was enabled to try a dodge on which I was very keen. I argued that since only a few weeks earlier I had been caught in Lübeck, the Germans would naturally tend to concentrate their search there. To ensure that they did so, when buying my ticket I mispronounced the name, gave the booking-office clerk the wrong coin, and was very rude to her. In short, I did everything possible to impress on her memory that a very strange foreigner was going to Lübeck. The balloon was not due to go up till 9 a.m. If I made my connection I should arrive there at 8 a.m. A supplementary ticket on, and by the time my trail had been followed through the suspicious ticket collector at Tarmstedt and the enraged girl at Bremen, I should be the best of fifty kilometres farther on towards Rostock.

A train did come in for Hamburg at 4.25, but it was the four o'clock express, which was running late. There are in Germany two kinds of train: Personenzugs, which are the slow locals, stopping at every halt; and D-Zugs, the fast non-stop expresses. The former were crowded with workmen and were not examined by the special police, while the latter, which often crossed old international frontiers, were subject to strict inspection. For this reason, unless there were urgent reasons to the contrary, all escapers normally kept to the slow trains. As I had to make my Hamburg connection, I decided to risk it and take the express. In the lavatory, I disposed of my tweed 'trousers' and put on the Merchant Navy buttons and cap badge.

As the train arrived in Hamburg the station loudspeakers were announcing the departure and platform of the Lübeck–Güstrow–Stettin train. A change from one side of the platform to the other, with no barriers to pass, and that evil bottle-neck of Hamburg was left behind. Fortune was with me and my hopes began to run high.

At Lübeck things went according to plan. The train waited ten minutes giving me time to get a ticket on to Rostock, and by eleven o'clock I was there.

On arrival I received a first-class shock. Ahead of me, going through the barrier, was an Unteroffizier from the interrogation camp. I am certain he did not see me; in fact the odds were that he would not have recognized me if he had, but it impressed me how much the escaper depends on his fortune. No foresight on God's earth can ensure against such chance encounters, and many is the escaper who has suffered an ill-deserved reverse through just that kind of bad luck.

It was at Rostock that David Jolly's maps stood me in good stead, for the docks were some distance from the railway station. I was full of hope as I walked to them, for I had always had a feeling that Rostock might bring me success. My arrival showed how inaccurate intuitions can be, for in the very short waterfront there were only a couple of German coasters and a Danish tramp.

I went to a crowded restaurant for lunch. As usual, it was a dreary business. There were so many people that only those who shouted loudest got anything to eat, and I could not afford to create a scene. Equally, to sit patiently for hours without getting anything would also cause suspicion. Eventually they brought me the stammgericht – a foul bowl of watery potato soup, but my first hot food for twenty-four hours.

After lunch I walked to the station to find out about a train for Stettin. I decided to take the Warnemunde–Rostock–Berlin express as far as Neu-Brandenburg and there spend the night. But I still had two hours to put in, and one of the biggest strains on an escaper is that he can never afford to be idle. Loungers and drifters are suspect, so he must always move as though he has an important appointment round the next corner. To do this for hours on end, in a greatcoat, is very wearying on the feet.

It was a real pleasure to travel again in a third-class compartment with cushioned seats after so much of the Continental wooden-bench style. Neu-Brandenburg produced quite a decent stamm, and I had a good night's rest there – but not this time in the Wehrmachtsunterkunft!

The next day dawned, Saturday the 12th February. I had a curious feeling that if I survived 3 p.m. – the 'arrest time' of my previous attempt – all would be well. I arrived at Stettin Hauptbahnhof at 9 a.m. to find it considerably altered. Where two months previously had been a large and bustling main station there now stood a wooden booking-office, a barrier of palings, and some rather precipitous platforms. No other building in the neighbourhood was damaged, which spoke well for the R.A.F. raid of 4th January.

From 9 a.m. till 1 p.m. I searched the docks, but my luck was right out. Not a Swedish ship could I find anywhere. After lunch I continued, but with no better fortune. Finally, just before 'arrest time', I went into a pub for a beer and to rest my feet. It was a rest that nearly cost me my freedom.

I slipped down to the bathroom to have a wash. I had, earlier in the morning, removed my 'scabs' as being no longer necessary, but in the course of doing so I must have removed a bit of genuine skin from my forehead, for on my coming back to my beer someone turned to me and said: 'Excuse me, sir, do you know your face is pouring with blood?' Sure enough, the side of my temple was all sticky, the very last thing I wanted; for it made me thoroughly conspicuous, when my whole object in life was to remain a nonentity.

I returned to the bathroom to staunch the bleeding. Rather shaken, I dropped my pocket-mirror and it rolled under the partition into an adjoining place. It took me several minutes to retrieve it and to get a bit of sticking-plaster on. Just as I was finishing, the man who had told me I was bleeding came to see if I was all right. Out of nothing more than politeness he mentioned that I did not sound German; where did I come from? I told him I was a Swede.

'Oh,' he said, breaking into Swedish, 'how nice to meet you. Where do you come from? I know Sweden very well – lived there ten years.'

I understood him well enough, but not having spoken the language for six years hardly dared vouchsafe a reply. A rather emaciated '*Jo*' was all that came out. He seemed hurt, and said something else I could not follow. But it was getting too hot for me, and muttering an apology I fled.

The proprietor looked at me strangely as I gulped down the rest of my beer and rushed out. I must admit that I was badly shaken and had somewhat lost my presence of mind. Once in the street my head cleared. Entering the next pub, I changed into the civilian buttons and took off my cap. A quick scrape with a razor, and my eyebrows, which normally meet in the middle, separated. The bleeding having stopped, I was able to take off my conspicuous patch.

Although my man was obviously suspicious, it might be some time before he thought of going for the police. There would be a further delay before they had patrols out. I would catch the next train out of town. Once clear of Stettin it should be safe enough; for there were too many strange types in Germany for them to follow up every clue.

Ten minutes later I arrived at the station – no special police at the barrier. The next train left for Danzig in ten minutes time. I bought a ticket there, and with a prayer of thanks boarded the train. It was 4.10, and 'arrest hour' was over. While waiting for the train to go I looked idly at my ticket. *It was 369 kilometres to Danzig* – the number I had selected for my pass.

At Belgard, an hour out of Stettin, I stopped for dinner. The stamm was, I considered, so important for the maintenance of strength and morale that I always broke my journey for it. Belgard turned out to be a good choice. There was a 'wash-and-brush-up' place, where for thirty pfennigs I was able to have a decent hot-water shave instead of a snow 'scrape' as hitherto.

At my table, while I was slowly eating, five Frenchmen joined me. Four were dressed in the Lincoln green of the so-called 'free' workers, and one, a much older man, was dressed as a civilian.

Starved of intercourse for three days, I joined in their conversation. The older man, one of those cosmopolitan and intelligent Frenchmen, was much interested in conditions in Sweden. I extemporized, reeling out such shortages as I remembered from England. Unfortunately, one of those I mentioned was matches, and my Frenchman, remembering Kruger, was quick to query this. I retrieved the situation by explaining that it was due to a shortage of sulphur.

They then began to ask my views on the war and Germany. Feeling that this was dangerous ground, I was noncommittal. I was longing with all my heart to cry out *'Vive L'Entente cordiale!'* but instead had to say how well the Germans had treated me. Not wishing to leave them too flat, I added cautiously that from a neutral vantage-point it looked as though things might be over in the course of the year That was too much for them.

One said in a loud voice: 'I knew it. You dislike the swine as much as we do. *Ces sales Boches sont haïts partout.*' Our table was surrounded by solid, bald-headed Prussians, and this remark terrified me. If but one of them understood French we might all find ourselves locked up. I had to remind my friends rather primly that I was neutral and could not agree with their remarks. As soon as possible I paid my bill and left. Later that evening I went on as far as Köslin, where I spent the night in a comfortable waiting-room.

The next day, 13th February, was a Sunday, and since a solitary figure walking round the docks might look suspicious, there being no work in progress, I took the train as far as the next big town – Stolp. After wandering around there for a bit I found a church and went inside. My reasons were two-fold. In the first place, I had much to be thankful for and was particularly anxious not to miss Mass. Secondly, and a more mundane reason, was that it was far the safest place to be.

It was also infinitely pathetic. The service was, of course, the same as would have been going on at home; the congregation was there for much the same reasons; the aged, the widowed, and the distressed were only too evident. The result was to give one a strange feeling of brotherhood with the enemy. Despite war, revolutions, and ten years of the Gestapo, the Church was still quietly carrying on her business as she had done in the Catacombs. I came out feeling strangely akin to the Germans. We had worshipped the same God in the same church – and the bonds of that mystical union were very real. Then there was a blare of trumpets, and a Hitler Youth contingent marched past. *Their* religion was one of brute national·force – it was a harsh return to the realities of life.

As I got back to the station a train drew in. The last carriage carried a placard saying 'Nur für Polen' (only for Poles). Out of it shuffled some starved-looking people dressed, for the most part, in sacking. Some of them went into the third-class waiting-room. I went too, for the mid-day stamm, and was treated with rough arrogance, so I moved to the second class, where such lower forms of life were not allowed and where I was fawned upon with obsequious civility.

It was 6.30 p.m. when I arrived in Danzig. The Haupt-bahnhof was thronged with a seething mass of people, like Paddington on a Bank Holiday. The waiting-room was so full that I despaired of even getting a beer. A more cogent objection to it was that there were some sharp-eyed station police about, which rendered the place unsuitable for spending the night.

I went out to find the streets crowded. A thaw had just set in, which made sleeping out of doors impossible, since it would dirty my clothes. I did not at this juncture wish to get captured experimenting with hotels, so I wandered round looking for shelter. I walked for three hours, but could find nothing, and in despair turned my steps in the direction of the station again.

On my way back I passed a building. A gust of warm air came through the door, and there were sounds of music and singing within. I thought how often, going to 'The Four Hun-dred' or the 'Savoy', I had paid but scant attention to the home-less on the pavement, to those poor wretches trying to get a night's rest on the Embankment. Now I was one of those 'on the outside, always looking in'. A big city can be very heartless. I hope I gained in humanity on this night; I certainly gained in experience.

I was dead tired when I got back to the station. Worse, I had only six marks left, and would have to conserve my funds. I found that I could get a return ticket for 1.50 Rm. on the District Line to a place called Gutenhafen. Trains ran every half-hour, and I resolved to go there for a good night's rest. The train was crowded with German sailors. By the time it left they were sitting on each other's knees and the corridor was packed. I thought nothing of this, till, arriving at the station, I found about ten naval policemen with gaiters and revolvers. Suddenly it occurred to me that Gutenhafen was the German name for Gdynia. I later learnt that about ninety per cent of the German Navy was congregated there on that particular night. Anyway it was no place for Lieutenant D. James, R.N.V.R., and I caught the next train back to Danzig.

I had, in the end, to spend the night in the main station. Before doing so, I took the precaution of looking at a telephone directory and scribbling the Swedish Consul's name and address on my passport. When the station police came round I told them that I had just arrived off the midnight train, that it

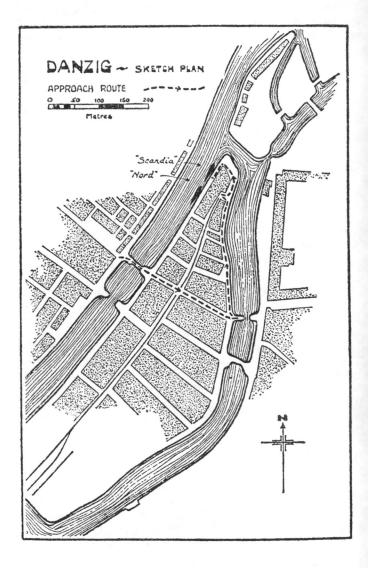

DANZIG ~ SKETCH PLAN

APPROACH ROUTE - - - -→

0   50   100   150   200
Metres

"Scandia"
"Nord"

N

was too late to go to the Consulate, and that I intended to stay where I was till morning. This satisfied them. Another symptomatic trait of the German police was that as long as one took a high-handed and slightly superior line with them they were far less trouble than if one was nervous.

Next morning, fortified by a cup of acorn coffee, I set off for the docks. Danzig is a large town, and I had only a rough notion where to go, so I used my little compass. Heading due east, I soon hit off some warehouses, and turning down-river I followed them for about two miles. At no point, however, was I able to penetrate the area. Every gate had a policeman on it, and from the noise inside I appeared to be going along behind shipbuilding yards.

Beginning to get very footsore, I retraced my steps to the station. On previous occasions I had had a beer and read the daily paper in a café whenever I wanted a rest from my continuous 'purposeful walking'. Now my funds were too low, and I was forced to go and sit in the lavatory for an hour. I was getting tired and feeling low and depressed. I began to think I would never find a ship, and felt very lonely.

On the next search, hitting the river at the same point, I turned up it and soon the building yards gave way to open quays. The river got smaller and smaller. Suddenly on rounding a corner, I saw a sight that made me blink, for a large ship appeared to be planted in the middle of Danzig.

I had come to a most fascinating part of the town. On either side of the river were high-gabled houses built of seventeenth-century brick. On my bank the ground-floor rooms of the houses consisted of little shops and cafés, with low oak beams. In front was a narrow cobbled road where fish vendors sold their wares off barrows. Beyond a low parapet lay the river, with small fishing-craft alongside. On the far bank stood tall granaries with gabled overhangs, looking like a print of Pepys' Thames, and there, incongruous but with that tang of glamour which is always attached to them, lay two big tramps, with tall stacks and rusty topsides. Each was flying a Danish ensign, and they were called *Scandia* and *Nord*.

Farther up-stream there was a bridge, and as I crossed it I could see the inevitable field-grey sentry patrolling between the gangways of the two ships. Going farther down the road I found that the river divided into two just below the Danish ships. They were in reality lying alongside an island. On the farther arm there were no ships, but I followed the road for another mile in case I came to any other tributaries. Finally, I retraced my footsteps in search of lunch.

Danzig in the spring of 1944 had an atmosphere quite unlike that of any other German town I visited. It was not unlike that of Edinburgh, for both had been left untouched by the destruction of war. Like Edinburgh, Danzig had been, during the course of five years' hostilities, the recipient of about four bombs, of which the inhabitants were inordinately proud. There was just that little bit more in the shop windows, too, and an outward air of prosperity, though in the case of Danzig this was largely fictitious, for their wares were only for display.

As I walked up the broad, cobbled streets, with their set-back painted façades and with trams squeezing under the low brick arches, I found it hard to believe that this was the match that had set Europe alight. The only reminder of war was the current anti-espionage campaign. In every shop window, on every page of every paper, was the silhouette of a sinister figure in black. These were displayed throughout the whole of Germany and afforded me particular pleasure, for I, too, was dressed completely in black, and hitherto nobody had attempted to stop me.

Near the station I found a very nice little restaurant. My beer was brought to me in a litre mug instead of the usual tooth-glass, and a waiter in tails showed me with deference to a sofa table. There were well-dressed people about, including girls with make-up. All this was quite unlike anything else I had seen in Germany, and even the bowl of stamm tasted better. If anyone cares to spend a week travelling third class, sleeping every night in the Paddington waiting-room, and then goes to, say, Claridge's, he will readily understand my sudden upwelling of spirits.

In the afternoon I resolved to carry my search farther afield. Walking down to the docks I overtook a French P.O.W. in a comparatively empty street. I stopped him and asked for a match. While he was producing it I told him hurriedly who I was and asked his advice on where I should find a ship. He showed no surprise, but directed me to the French stevedores' camp some two miles distant. He said they would put me up, feed me, and find me a suitable ship in due course. Then, with a *'Vivent les Alliés!'* he was gone.

Walking to the camp, my feet grew increasingly sore. It needed a great effort of will not to limp, but I thought I might cause suspicion. Nearing the French camp I fell in with two more Frenchmen. Their welcome was less friendly. They assured me that it was impossible to keep me in their camp, for things had been tightened up. As for Swedish ships – that, too, was very difficult. No, they knew of none at that minute. Had I tried the workmen in the goods yard? Perhaps they could help. Where could I sleep? There was a good hay-barn down the road, about a mile away, on the left-hand side.

Suddenly I realized that I was almost beyond making it. I had enough money left for one meal. I could go to the barn hungry and have a feed next morning, or I could have a hot dinner that evening and look forward to nothing later. It was well below freezing-point again, so it was doubtful whether I could last longer than one more day. It seemed highly doubtful whether this extra day would materially alter the shipping situation. But I could reasonably expect help aboard one of the Danish ships, and there was no logical reason why they should not be going to Sweden. I decided it would be better to board one that evening, while I still had sufficient reserves of strength, rather than to wait an extra day, when fatigue and cold might well reduce me below the level of taking adequate precautions.

I know now that I could have found Swedish ships within three miles if I had only known where to look for them. My advance information had been, however, nil. No plan of escape is without risks. It is a matter of objectively weighing relative disadvantages. A slightly more dangerous course may well be the best if it preserves strength and will-power, which are dependent ultimately on physical condition. One views oneself with curious detachment, escaping. The body, like identity papers, money, and clothes, is one of the instruments of action. One judges almost dispassionately the stresses to which it can be put, as though it were a car or marine engine.

The definite decision to board a ship was a relief and a tonic. There were still about three hours till darkness, so I decided to go to a cinema, and found one which opened at 4 p.m. and was showing a musical comedy – just the thing. But I had reckoned without the behaviour of German crowds. A quarter of an hour before the curtain went up the booking-office was a sea of jostling humanity. Middle-aged, bald, and bull-necked Prussians were getting their heads down in the scrum, while their wives screamed abuse at each other and at the police. Four uniformed policemen tried to keep order. It became evident that there would soon be arrests, and since I could not afford to be implicated, I gave up the struggle and drifted away. I had not enough money to sit and drink, so I had to put in another couple of hours' walking.

At dusk I went back to my lunch-time restaurant for a last meal. Since the Germans would obviously sit heavily on me if they caught me again, I decided to give them as little pretext as possible. Roddy had been given seven days' extra cells for possessing money. I resolved to spend all I had left, also to dispose of my identity papers, so that I could not be had up for 'forgery'.

In the café the head waiter recognized me and took me to my old table. There were two girls opposite who behaved as though they were members of the frail sisterhood. Their appetites were anything but frail. They ordered four plates of soup and four tellergerichte (the couponed dish of the day). This caused the waiter no surprise. He duly put four soups in front of them. When they had finished the first bowl, the second was placed on top of it and likewise emptied. The same was done with the meat course. It was a strange performance for two well-dressed girls. I can only assume that they had just got their new books of coupons and were out to make a night of it. Anyway, I took the tip and ordered two stamms.

These, with their accompanying beers, left me with thirty-five pfennigs, which I gave to the waiter. I then went to the bathroom and changed my collar and tie for a polo-necked sweater, for I wanted no light colours in case they showed up. I was just going to destroy my identity papers when I thought I might be challenged on the way down to the wharf, so I kept them.

My plan was to go down along the back of the spit and try to board one of the ships from the seaward end. I would walk boldly down, and if there was a sentry there – which was most unlikely, for there was nothing for him to guard – I could explain that I was out for a stroll. Once at the end of the wharf my movements would perforce become suspicious, so I would destroy my identity papers as giving me no further protection.

I passed the turning so that I could view the road from the bridge. Stopping to tie my shoe-lace on the parapet, I looked round carefully, but saw nothing, so turned back and walked swiftly down to the wharves. No sentry stopped me, and I soon reached a blind alley just short of the last warehouse. There was a police boat, with a searchlight, moving about lower down the river, and I decided to wait as long as I could. Moonrise was at 9.30p.m., and I should have to board one of the tramps before then. It was reasonable to assume that the sentry would change at 9 p.m. – the standard German hour – so I planned to slip on board as soon as his relief arrived and before his eyes were used to the dark. At that moment the clocks chimed 7.15.

My alley-way was bare and muddy; the only cover in it a corner of deep shadow. I was confident that an unsuspecting man could walk by within a few inches without seeing me. I spent the first half-hour eating my identity papers. Then I blacked my face and hands with a light wash of mud and put my wrist-watch in my pocket so that there was no chance of the luminous dial being seen. Finally, I took off my shoes and hung them round my neck, so that I could beat a noiseless retreat if anyone came.

It was a cold and cheerless place to wait, especially as a prelude to the final and all-important step. The tall, grim warehouses were silent, yet to my strained nerves alive with noise. A rat scuttled by. My stockinged feet in two inches of soft and near-frozen mud got very cold.

I reflected that a year previously I had been sitting comfortably in the Mess at Felixstowe. If anyone had then suggested to me that I should one day crawl about on hands and knees in an enemy seaport I should have thought him crazy. It was a fantastic and bizarre situation. A nearby church clock chimed the quarters. It was very like the old clock in Lupton's tower at Eton. I thought of the river and the 4th of June – Hubert Hartley going down the towpath on his bicycle, so keen on watching his four that he rode over a courting couple on the edge of the towpath without ever realizing it. Someone told him about it after the race, and he immediately rode off to apologize, like the good fellow he is. Two of Eton's finest captains of boats, who won the school-pulling my first half, were killed in the Battle of Britain – Jimmie Barker and David Bury – 'others will take our places, dressed in the old light blue' – sung by a thousand young voices in the minor key – an unforgettable memory. It was less than a year since my last hunt with the Grafton – Will Pope and the whipper-in still in tattered pink, though the lights of Europe were out; the field, half a dozen farmers, a few children, and a couple of officers on leave. Hounds found quickly, and only Will Pope, the Secretary's daughter, a farmer, and myself got away. They ran fast for just on an hour and we had them all to ourselves. A month later and I was sitting in Germany. . . .

Approaching footsteps ended my reverie, but they came from the opposite bank of the river, carrying far over the water in the still night air. It was ten to nine, and I would have to be off.

The spit had a squared end about fifty yards long. The jetty was flanked by the bare walls of the warehouses on one side and mooring bollards on the other. It seemed fearfully light and there was no cover, but keeping well into the wall I crept to the corner.

When I reached it I could hear the steady clump, clump of the sentry's boots coming towards me. A dozen paces off they turned, and as soon as they began to recede I poked my head round. My object was to avoid silhouetting myself against the calm water, and for that I had to keep as low as possible.

The situation, on which everything hung, immediately appeared favourable. Fifteen feet away the stern of the *Scandia* loomed high and sinister. Her mooring wires were too loose to render swarming feasible, but a ladder rose almost vertically from the quay to her bridge, and there was a little cover at its foot in the lee of a large bollard.

But best was the fact that the sentry, now a hundred yards away, was shining a torch, which would certainly deprive his eyes of night vision for everything beyond its range. Keeping well into the wall, I ran down the quay and jinked over behind the bollard. The sentry was still patrolling towards the other ship, but had evidently heard a noise, for he turned and flashed his torch in my direction. I was still beyond its feeble ray – twenty seconds later I was on the lower bridge of the *Scandia*.

There was no one on deck, and the companionway leading down to the engine-room was open. I went down and for'ard through an alleyway between the boilers to the stoke-hold. Opening the door of one of the fires, I rejoiced in the first real and glowing warmth I had experienced for several days. I then passed through into the bunkers. For'ard of the stoke-hold they extended across the full beam of the ship, and a narrow wing bunker, five feet broad, flanked the engine-room and boiler-room on either side. Above these wings there were 'tween-deck bunkers, which consisted only of narrow plate ledges two feet wide, with a gap between. She was very low in coal. At no point was it stacked more than eight feet high.

Hearing a noise where I had warmed myself, I looked back through one of the traps, to see a man banking up for the night. I had to take a chance and find out where the ship was going, and I went through and told him who I was. He seemed incredulous at first, so I produced my P.O.W. identity disc and the letter with its English stamp. Believing me at length, he took a quick look into the engine-room to see that the coast was clear. That looked good. He then told me that the ship was loading grain for Lübeck and would next take coal up to North Denmark. He did not yet know which Danish port it would be, but thought they should be there within ten days. He added that I could stay and he would feed me, as long as no one else knew that I was on board. If I were found I would naturally say that I had received no help. With that, for he was very nervous, he left me, returning a few minutes later to say that the ship was moving to another berth at six o'clock next morning and sailing at noon the day after. He advised me to hide in one of the wing bunkers.

Although North Denmark was not ideal for my purpose, I accepted the offer. It was certainly a healthier spot for Englishmen than North Germany, and there was always a chance of getting help for the remaining stage of my journey to Sweden. The only alternative would have been to give myself up. So, removing the more jagged bits of coal, I made myself a bed in the bunkers and was soon sound asleep.

I was awakened next morning by the engine-room telegraphs

as the ship moved down-river to her new berth, but throughout that day – Monday – I was undisturbed. In the evening my stoker friend, Johannsen was his name, brought me a packet of three sandwiches and a pint bottle of acorn coffee. It was my first food for twenty-four hours, and turned out to be my daily ration for the next five days, for he could not risk bringing me more. Curiously enough, although I looked forward to it eagerly as the one break in the day's dark monotony, I never felt hunger – only, towards the end, a growing thirst.

Early on Tuesday, Johannsen came down and completely buried me in coal, lest there should be a Customs search. My face had to be left above the surface so that I could breathe, but it was three-quarters surrounded by the side of the ship and by a large Z-shaped angle frame. I was also warned on no account to reveal my presence to the trimmer, a boy of about eighteen, who had leanings towards Nazi doctrines.

It is not nice being buried under coal. Even a couple of inches of it sits surprisingly heavily on the stomach, and it is impossible to move so much as a muscle. Added to all this, I was lying along the ship's side so as to gain the protection of the frame, and, being below the water-line, it was very cold. I could not see my watch, neither could I smoke.

About 4 p.m., by which time I deduced from the rhythmic heaving of the hull that we were well out of the river and in open water, I decided that eight hours' burial was more than enough and it was high time I emerged. I had just wiggled my head clear when the trimmer came to my wing of the bunker, bringing with him a hurricane-lamp on a flexible lead. He hung it so that the beam fell just below my chin. The coal on my chest was brilliantly lit, but my face was still in shadow. He began digging so close to me that I was afraid he might uncover my arm, or even cut it with his shovel. I lay absolutely still.

After a couple of minutes he stopped for a breather. As he leant on his shovel, his face was within two feet of mine. I could see the pulse beating in his temple. Both his breath and his feet smelt foul. It is strange to look a man straight in the face and find that he cannot see you. I was so certain that he must have that I began to think of explanations, but some inner instinct warned me to play 'possum. The contrast between a harsh white light and a corner of shadow in black coal is very great, and he apparently had no suspicions. I shut my eyes, and after an anxious minute heard him go off elsewhere.

I now developed my bunker 'routine'. The trimmer was a 'day-man', and, therefore, no cause for fear at night, so by day I used to lie in the 'tween-deck bunkers, which were empty, and come down on to the coal for 'dinner' and 'bed'.

One develops a curious mentality under such circumstances. At one end of the bunker there was a large, flat bit of coal which I thought of as the 'dining-room'. Grave was my anger when the dining-room table was shovelled through to the stoke-hole by the relentless trimmer. At the other end an area of soft coal-dust made my 'bedroom'. I used to spend about an hour every evening 'making my bed' – that is to say, finding a suitable patch, removing all the uncomfortable lumps, and filling the holes with coal-dust. This job had to be done daily; for the contours were continually changing as my home was fed through to the boilers.

In the 'tween-deck bunkers I had to exercise the most consummate care lest any noise should be transmitted through to the engine-room. Another source of anxiety was a cough, which was growing steadily worse. It was often a real struggle to keep it under control for the hour or so that the trimmer was working underneath me.

Apart from the big moment each evening when I was brought food, my only relaxation was smoking. Knowing their importance to morale, I had brought over two hundred cigarettes hidden in my clothes. Provided no one was about, I smoked one every hour and a half. This made the passage of time seem significant in the darkness, and went far to help me keep a balanced and cheerful outlook.

On Friday evening, 18th February, we docked in Lübeck, and the following morning the ship bunkered, giving me a merry old time dodging wayward bits of coal that ricochetted in my direction. In the evening Johannsen came to me and said that the ship's sailing had been changed. She was due to return in ballast to Königsberg, and from there to take grain on to Bremen. I had by this time been sitting for five days in pitch darkness on a low diet, and it was beginning to pall. Now that the *Scandia* was no further use to me, it was obvious that I should have to find another ship, sooner or later, and the only question was where – Lübeck or Königsberg?

Lübeck presented many advantages. I knew it well from my previous visit, and the geography was fairly simple. Moreover, Johannsen had seen a Swedish ship sail up-river that afternoon, so I had a definite objective to make for. In the back of my mind, too, I always put faith in the German who had told me in the cells of the forty-eight hours' sailing from the SVEA Line wharf. A further advantage was that if I were caught I could be assured of reasonable treatment from the Lübeck Wassers-schutzpolizei and should not have too long a train journey back to the camp.

I came up on deck at about 11 p.m. for what was to be my last and most fascinating night in Germany. It was good to breathe fresh air again, and the night was exhilarating; for it was freezing very hard and lacked but four days till the full moon.

The ship was lying alongside a vast elevator discharging grain. There were four railway tracks and some open ground between the ship's side and the elevator, and the area was lit by arc-lights. A sentry was patrolling up and down this floodlit zone.

As it grew colder, towards midnight, the sentry tended to slip inside the doorway of the elevator every now and then to warm his hands, and though he never went far in – I could always see the back of his coat – his visits grew longer and longer.

Eventually I decided that on his next entrance I would make a dash for it. If he saw me it was unlikely that with frozen fingers and a rifle at 'safe' he would be able to hit a moving body, and his eyes would be unused to the dark. On the other hand, he would probably give the alarm, so I hoped to get away unobserved. As soon as he went in I jumped over the ship's side and ran. Reaching shadow, I waited till he came out and was quite certain from his demeanour that he had seen nothing. I looked at my watch. It was just after midnight of Sunday, 20th February.

I soon established from the Pole Star that I was somewhere in the lower reaches of the river, two or three miles outside Lübeck. I started walking, therefore, up the western bank, looking for ships. After half a mile of easy going over hard, frozen ground I smelt that lovely and quite unmistakable clean, fresh smell of timber, and knowing that Sweden exported a lot of softwood to Germany I climbed a low wall to investigate, and found myself in a timber yard. There lay a large ship with a deck cargo and a Swedish name on her bow.

I could hear a sentry's boots squeaking up and down, but could not pick him out against the background of stacked lumber. Arguing that if I could not see him he would certainly fail to spot me if I made no noise, I took off my shoes and crept aboard.

There was no trace of the ship's port of registry on her life-belts or lifeboats, but there were sounds of a party coming from the saloon amidships. I tiptoed stealthily to the door and put my ear to the keyhole. The voices within were drunken and confused, but after a minute or two I made out that some of them were Finnish . . . so she was no good to me.

Going ashore again, I continued in stockinged feet through deserted piles of timber, feeling ever more strongly the bizarre nature of the situation. A few hundred yards farther on I found a Swedish ship, again with a deck cargo, but I was forced, albeit reluctantly, to leave her, for she was only a small auxiliary schooner and would have nowhere to hide me while discharging.

I was now getting into the town proper, and for an hour picked my way through a confused labyrinth of docks, warehouses, and railways. I moved quietly, and hid whenever I saw anyone coming, but there were not many people abroad at two in the morning.

At one point I climbed on to the low penthouse roof of a shed and followed it along for several hundred feet. At the end I lowered myself down by my hands and let go, expecting a drop of a few inches. I fell about ten feet, fortunately without hurting myself. Heights are difficult to judge in the dark. In the yard thus gained was a German 'M' class mine-sweeper, which was, curiously enough, quite unguarded. It would have been easy for a saboteur to have boarded her, but for me there was no point in that, so I went on.

Finally, after nearly losing myself in a maze of streets, I arrived at the main bridge crossing the river. Just by the

Halbinsel gate, where I had been caught the time before, the air-raid sirens went, and as the Germans do not allow people in the streets during an alert, I was forced to lie up underneath a lorry.

After days of being cooped up, I had so much enjoyed this crazy round of exploration that I had had no opportunity to think. I now had leisure to see that my position was far from rosy. My shoes were hanging round my neck. I was pitch black and my clothes were in rags. By my watch it was four o'clock. As soon as daylight came I should assuredly be finished. For that matter, if anyone were to stop me before daylight my chances would be slim. I had no papers, and no story could adequately explain my state. My only hope would be to pretend to be drunk.

I even debated going to the Wasserschutzpolizei and giving myself up. It would be fun to see their faces when I knocked at the door, and I would be given a bath and a bed with mattress and blankets. . . . I had forty cigarettes left. Were I captured it would take two days for an escort from the camp to get up to fetch me and a further two days before I got back . . . ten cigarettes a day that meant . . . hello! the All Clear and the time 4.30. Still a couple of hours to go. I would go to the SVEA wharf first, and if I drew blank there go back to the Halbinsel, hide my greatcoat and case, and attempt to board a ship in daylight as though I were a trimmer.

The SVEA wharf was, as I knew, opposite the police station.* I was anxious lest there should be a policeman on guard at the door, who might recognize me, but not a sign of life showed itself there. Better still, there was a large passenger-type vessel at the quay and no sentry on her gangway. I went aboard.

From the first she was a mystery ship. There was no trace of a name on her bow or counter, nor was there any on her lifebelts or lifeboats. But for the evident fact that she had steam up and that there was an ensign hanging limply astern, I doubt whether I would have stayed aboard. On the other hand, what lent confirmation to my German's story of a mail service to Gothenburg was that she was remarkably like a passenger vessel

* See sketch-plan facing p. 117.

– that is to say, all her deck-houses were amidships, she had a raised boat-deck, and was beautifully kept.

I tried all the cabin doors on the upper deck, but they were locked. I went into the chart-house and used up my remaining matches trying to see what she was from her documents, but they were locked too. Finally, and in desperation, as dawn was beginning to break, I went after and hauled down the ensign to try to find her nationality, but it was still too dark to see.

This last manoeuvre was watched from the jetty by a sentry recently returned to his post. One of the jokes about stalking a ship is that no matter what risks are involved in getting aboard, once there one can lean over the rail and cock snooks at any sentry. One is merely assumed to be a member of the ship's company.

If there had been no sentry there – funny thought – I think I should have left the ship after this last failure to establish her identity. But I was forced to stay, and in doing so found out her secret; for passing a door I had not been able to see an hour earlier, I heard snores coming from within, and on opening it I saw a night watchman sound asleep, with a peculiar type of Finnish seaman's knife lying by his side.

It was too late to find another ship. I had to take a chance on this one. Getting well into shadow, so that he should not see my face, I banged on the door. Out he came, rubbing the sleep out of his eyes. To make sure that he did not speak it well, I said to him, '*Sprechen Sie Deutsch?*' '*Nein.*' I asked him in Finnish whether he spoke Swedish – yes, a little. Finally, in as haughty a tone as I could muster, I asked him in Swedish where his ship was bound for and what time she sailed.

'We sail for Stockholm, in an hour and a half's time, with two thousand tons of oranges,' came the reply, 'but (suspiciously) who are you?' It was my pleasure, since he spoke no German, to reply 'German Customs'. To take my captor's name in vain at this juncture was indeed rich. . . .

It only remained to utilize this astonishing stroke of fortune. I found my way down various steep ladders to the stoke-hold and started groping around. A light went on, and I was confronted by a tough little stoker. Simply, and in Swedish, I told him who I was and what I wanted, and stressed the fact of my year in the Finnish Merchant Service and my regard for Finns.

I awaited his reply. It was an anxious moment. He scrutinized me carefully and then replied in broken English: 'I like England. I had one plenty good girl in Hull. Very nice, but we have war. Plenty risky take you across.' I felt that the moment had come for a bribe, since the German search party might be expected on board at any minute.

The British Government always made it clear that they would honour any 'reasonable' sum offered by prisoners in their attempts to get out. Unhappily no one had ever dared to lay down in black and white what constituted such a 'reasonable' bribe. I had heard every figure from £5 to £500 mentioned. Anyway, owing to the urgency of the situation, I was prepared to take no chance. I offered him £200 – the highest sum that I could afford to pay myself should the Government be unwilling to fork out so much. For him it would represent about two years' wages – a substantial inducement, but not too much in view of the risk to his life.

For a minute he hesitated – then he asked me to write down my name and address. The battle was won. It was now up to him to find a sufficiently good hiding spot. He said that he had just the place for me – underneath the boilers. Taking me into the alley-way, he unscrewed a manhole, and shining a toch within, told me to worm my way into the space between Nos. 1 and 2 boilers.

It was a hard struggle getting underneath the boiler, and despite the asbestos lagging it was very hot. I came to the angle between the two boilers, and there I hid. Behind me I could hear my little friend screwing down the manhole. . . .

A few minutes later I heard the heavy-nailed boots of soldiery ringing on the metal floors. I had every sort of fear. My cough was getting worse, and it was only with difficulty that I could control it. Ten days had passed since last I had a bath or changed my shirt, and I even feared that they might smell me. I could hear them lifting up several of the engine-room floorplates, then the crunch of their boots as they raked through the coals. They tapped around the boiler casing behind which I was hiding, but they never looked within. . . .

As soon as we sailed, the temperature rose alarmingly and a new terror assailed me. What proof had I that it was possible to maintain life under a ship's boilers at all? Was my stoker acting in good faith? The Finns, although charming people, are of non-European Mongol stock. It would be quite possible, psychologically, for a Finn to lure a man into such a situation in order to listen to his death agony. All my claustrophobia rose in support of such a notion. I was locked in . . . unable to do more than turn over . . . and it grew hotter and hotter and hotter.

Suddenly the engine-room telegraph rang down 'stop', and as the ship lost way I could hear the distant reverberations of her anchor cable running through the hawse-pipe. I groped round for my brief-case, which I had laid in the bilge; for I wanted something to protect my thigh from the angular pig-iron ballast on which I was lying. . . . I could not find it. . . . Instantly I guessed that that probably explained why we had stopped . . . it had been swept forward into the engine bilge and found by the searchers . . . they had deduced that this meant a stowaway and were coming down to fetch me . . . I could hear someone unscrewing the bolts of the manhole, a torch was shining in my direction . . . if I kept very low they might not see me. . . . A voice was saying in English: 'Are you all right?' . . .

I looked up to see a pleasant-faced Finn crawling under the boilers and saying, 'Gosh, it's ploddy hot down here.' All my fears and fantasies vanished. When he reached me he said that owing to British mine-laying planes we had to anchor for a couple of hours while the trawlers swept a channel. Yes, the Germans had left the ship, but I would have to stay where I was till we docked in Stockholm in two and a half days' time, for most of the crew were unreliable. But I need not worry, he and his friend – the one I met – were in the same watch and would look after me. I would probably be feeling hungry and thirsty, so he had brought me something. . . .

'Something' turned out to be two pint-bottles of water, bread and cheese, and six oranges. He told me that three watches of two stokers each kept standing watches. I would have to be shut down and very careful during the Forenoon and First (8–12 a.m. and p.m.), for they were 'no damn good man'; but his watch (12 till 4) and the Morning- and Dog-watchmen were all friends.

With this information he left me to settle down to sixty hours of hell. When first I arrived in the camp someone advanced the theory that we had all been killed in our various actions and were, though we did not realize it, in purgatory. It had always struck me as an amusing and original idea, and I could but now believe that I had descended one lower in the scale and gone to hell itself.

We sailed again about ten o'clock, and the fact that we were going over a minefield did nothing to increase my peace of mind. If we hit one, I could only hope to be killed outright rather than scalded to death when the boilers burst.

Although it was stiflingly hot, I found I could get a current of deliciously cool air if I kept my nose forward and well down on the bilge. But here another difficulty arose; for every few minutes the stokers would rake the embers out of the fires, whereupon flames would find their way uncomfortably close to me through the cracks in the casing. Then, when a bucket of water was thrown over them, my cubby-hole would be filled with steam, smuts, and bits of smouldering slag. Never have I been in surroundings more suggestive of the lower regions.

As soon as my friends came on watch the situation changed radically, for a small trap-door into the stokehold, which I had not hitherto noticed, was opened, and I was able to sit with my head through it and talk. Again, my resourceful friend produced a piece of duck-boarding six feet by two, which was passed through to me. This meant that I had something dry and smooth to lie on instead of ballast-pigs and icy bilge-oil. Finally, at 12.30, my dinner was brought to me. It consisted of the traditional thick pea-soup and salt pork, a bowl of duff, and two pints of milked and sugared coffee. For dessert there were as many oranges as I could possibly eat. It was my first really square meal for eleven days.

I will not weary the reader with any further description of the next two days. Many times I was tempted to give up and take a chance on the officers not handing me over to a German patrol vessel. The only thing that prevented me from doing so was that the first time I had made a muck of things through thinking myself safe too soon, and it would have been an ever-lasting cause for regret and shame if I had failed at this juncture through lack of guts.

Taking a lesson from the previous disappointment, I decided that I should not regard myself as safe until I actually made contact with the British Consul. I took all precautions. In case I should be caught leaving the ship and detained illegally, I gave my friend a note to take to the British Legation; while if I got ashore successfully we arranged he was to meet me the following evening at the Consulate for payment.

We docked at 3 p.m. on Shrove Tuesday, 22nd February. At the crew's request I did not go ashore till it was dark at 6 p.m., and that three hours' wait was the longest of the whole twelve days.

At 6 p.m. precisely, and just as I had finished my last cigarette from the camp, my friend opened up my hiding-place. Together we climbed the ladders to deck level. A quick reconnaissance and he gave two low whistles. I picked up my bag and went ashore.

Stockholm was very wintry after Germany. There was thick snow on the ground and large chunks of ice floated in the dock. But more inspiring was the feeling that I was in a land of friends. Everywhere, great neon signs met the eye. After four and a half years of black-out I will not attempt to describe my emotions.

I could not find my way out of the dockyard, but I fell in with two labourers going home. They offered to take me to the Customs House, and on the way there, struck no doubt by my singular appearance, they asked me who I was. As soon as I told them they both patted me on the back and shook me by the hand. One of them insisted on giving me ten kroner, or about fifteen shillings. The other gave me some sandwiches and oranges.

At the Customs House we rang up the Consul and the police. The Consul arrived first and assured me that all my troubles were over. The police would keep me for the night as a formality and release me the next day.

The police, who arrived by car to fetch me, insisted on driving down the famous 'Kungsgatan' to let me see the bright lights. When we arrived, I was first given a big supper and then interviewed by a charming plain-clothes man who spoke good English. Three policemen, armed with scrubbing brushes, finally combined to give me five baths, which removed most of the coal and the oil. I had no idea it was possible to be so dirty.

Next morning, in prison garb, I was driven to MEA, Stock-

133

holm's Army and Navy Stores, where I met Mr. Bernardes, the Vice-Consul, who helped me to buy a complete outfit of decent clothes. Afterwards he gave me an excellent lunch and took me down to the Legation.

It would be invidious to say who was kindest here; for everyone from the Minister himself down to the old hall porter went out of his way to be nice. The Naval Attaché, Captain H.M. Denham, R.N., gave me a diary when I went in to see him. He said that I should need it if I were to remember all my engagements, and he had taken the liberty of putting the first few in it . . . suffice it to say that I was dining with him that evening, lunching with the Minister next day, dining the same evening with Lieutenant Dan Gibson Harris, R.N.V.R., the Assistant Naval Attaché, and lunching the day after with Colonel Sutton Pratt, the Military Attaché. Coming out of the dark veil of misery which was Nazi Germany into the full sunlight of such kindness made me indeed proud and happy to be British.

But one thing remains to be said. It is the most important. Every escaper is agreed that the most vital factor involved is that of luck. Many first-class men, braver, more ingenious, and more pertinacious than I, tried many times, but never had the fortune to pull it off. Some of them, like Squadron-Leader Bushell and the forty-nine other martyrs of Sagan and like Lieutenant-Commander James Buckley, R.N., of the Fleet Air Arm, paid forfeit for their attempts with their lives. Even in my final and successful attempt I made three bad mistakes and yet got away with it. Why?

Every man I talked to who got home has told me that even in the darkest moment he was acutely aware of the help and guidance of some higher but personal Being. It is the same phenomenon as that experienced by Shackleton and his comrades crossing South Georgia in 1915, after their wonderful openboat journey from Elephant Island. Smythe reported a similar feeling when alone on the final pyramid of Everest. The scoffer, who denies the validity of this contention of personal guidance, is speaking on matters about which he has no experience. His objections, therefore, hold no validity. It is elementary knowledge that when the body is leading a somewhat ascetic existence, the spirit is more perceptive. Christian and Oriental ascetic mysticism for the last four thousand years have been based on that fact.

The cynic replies: 'It's all very well for you to speak; you had the luck; but what about those who failed? The whole thing is easily explained by the laws of average, whereby some-one sooner or later is bound to succeed.' On purely intellectual grounds that answer may suffice, but it is not one that would satisfy anybody who has experienced as well as thought about these things.

The only remaining question is – Why is it, if these matters are indeed of personal interest to the Almighty, that His selec-tion is so arbitrary? Why, if there are two women working in the fields, should the one be taken and the other left? That is, of course, quite unanswerable; for from our limited vantage-point we cannot see enough of the picture.

Anyway, enough of this philosophizing. Throughout the book I have endeavoured to give thanks to all those whose as-sistance was instrumental – nay, all-important – to my getting away. My object in the preceding paragraphs is to express my gratitude to the most important One of all. . . .

A few strands remain to be picked up. My Finnish friend duly came round to the Legation and was paid his £200, nor was I ever expected to pay any of it myself. I was at first anxious lest he should give himself away by the unwonted dis-play of so much money, but he convinced me that he would not do anything so silly. He had been carrying on a very lucra-tive three-way smuggling business between Germany, Sweden, and Finland ever since the war started. True, I was the first contraband livestock he had taken, but the principles involved were the same as for coffee or silks.

Twelve days after I arrived in Stockholm, two other R.N.V.R. Lieutenants, Dennis Kelleher of Combined Oper-ations and Stewart Campbell, Fleet Air Arm, both of Marlag, arrived there too, having followed much the same route, and they were able to tell me how my cover worked.

Apparently the Germans found that they were one short on my bath party and reported it to the Feldwebel of the watch. To make sure that they had not miscounted on the way up they held a tally appel. Warrant Officer James, R.A.F., who was much like me in build and colouring as well as in name, succeeded in passing the Germans twice – once with my tally and a naval greatcoat, and once with his own and an R.A.F. coat. If caught, he stood to get a heavy sentence in the cells, with no possible prospect of gain for himself. Without his cover I should never have got farther than Tarmstedt station.

How the Germans heard of my departure gave me endless pleasure. Apparently Jackson, posing as the French veterinarian, had very bad luck; for he tripped over a wire on the Swiss frontier and was recaptured the same day I made my break. The Germans had been getting increasingly worried about him for some days past; for with his perfect knowledge of German he was obviously a strong starter who might well blot their still clear copybook. Next morning, therefore, the Kommandant came into the camp, all smiles, and said to Commander Lambert, who had recently become man-of-confidence: 'Good morning, Kapitän Lambert, I am sure you will be glad to see your friend, Lieutenant Jackson, again. He has reported back from leave.' To which he got the reply: 'Good morning, Captain Bachausen. I'm sure you will be sorry not to see your friend Lieutenant James back again. He's just gone on leave!'

The day after my arrival in Stockholm was that on which the second reading of the Education Bill was brought up in the House of Commons. My father, as P.P.S. to the President of the Board, Mr. R. A. Butler, was sitting behind him with notes.

A slip of paper was handed to him and he read: 'Your son has succeeded in escaping from Germany and is now in Stockholm. He will be home shortly.' I gather he was not quite his normal and model P.P.S. self for the rest of the debate.

It was 4 a.m. on a cold morning some three weeks later when a Mosquito landed me at Leuchars. The Customs waved through the silk stockings and other presents I had for my family, and a Reception Officer told me I had a seat on the 10 a.m. 'Flying Scotsman' from Edinburgh. I put through a trunk call and got in touch with an aunt who was on night ambulance duty in London. I told her that I would arrive at 6.35 p.m.; would she let everyone know?

It would have taken the gilt off the gingerbread if they had had to wait two hours, but for once the train was dead on time.

At the barrier were seven members of the family, of whom three were up from the far ends of the country on compassionate leave. . . . One cannot be given many minutes such as that in a lifetime.

APPENDIX

Reference Sheet No. 734   SECRET

From ....Naval Attaché, Stockholm.
To ....Director of Naval Intelligence
Date ....15th March, 1944.

Subject: ESCAPE OF LIEUT. JAMES R.N.V.R.: FROM GERMANY

Attached is Lieut. James's account of his recent escape from Germany, where he was a prisoner of war, to Sweden. It is requested that a copy of this report should be forwarded to M.I.9.

Lieutenant James has made a most excellent impression on us in Stockholm, and I consider the account of his escape is a fine story of the resourcefulness to be expected of this young officer.

The key to this report will be forwarded under R.S. 734A. (attached).

H. M. DENHAM

CAPTAIN
NAVAL ATTACHE

From................Naval Attaché, Stockholm.
To..................Director of Naval Intelligence.
Date ....15 March, 1944.

Subject: ESCAPE OF LIEUT. JAMES R.N.V.R.: FROM
                GERMANY

Reference my R.S. 734 of today's date, key to the report is
attached herewith:

Sydney Horler ....Commander Beale, R.N.
Edgar Wallace ....S/Lt. R. F. Jackson, R.N.V.R.
Hobbs ....Lt. Rodwell, R.N.V.R.
Sutcliffe.............Lt. R. M. Eggleston, R.N.V.R.
Freeman ....⌐⌐Lt. Davis, R.N.V.R.
Hardy ....Lt. Balkwell, R.N.V.R.
Willis................W/O McFarlane, R.A.F.
Sherlock Holmes ......Lt. J. Pryor, R.N.
M. Hercule Poirot ....Lt. Com. A. Cheyne, R.N.
Mr. Rembrandt ......Lt. W. Hussey, R.N.V.R.
Dr. Crippen ....Lt. Comm. O. Sullivan, R.N.
Mr. Boris Karloff ....Dr. Knight and Lt. K. Cox, R.N.

                                    H. M. DENHAM

                                    CAPTAIN
                                    NAVAL ATTACHE

1. On 26th February, 1943, M.G.B. 79 under my command, was part of a unit under the command of Lt-Com. Hichens, D.S.O., D.S.C., R.N.V.R. Our orders were to escort a unit of M.L.s on a mine-laying operation and thereafter we had freedom of action off the Dutch Coast until dawn. We sailed from FELIXSTOWE at 1645. By 0100 27th February we had escorted the M.L.s clear of Dutch waters and shortly after parting company with them we encountered 3 German armed trawlers off IMUJDEN.

2. In the course of the ensuing engagement M.G.B. 79 received multiple hits aft, which put both main and emergency steering out of action as well as all lights, telegraphs, etc. While I was down in the engine room endeavouring to manoeuvre clear on main engines M.G.B. 79 was hit and set on fire in the tank space and having got out a distress signal both by wireless and by firing a Lewis-gun tracer vertically – a flotilla signal of great value in a Coastal craft engagement – we abandoned ship.

3. M.G.B.s 77 and 112 returned and succeeded in picking up part of the crew, but were then forced to retire. I had fully anticipated this decision and realized the necessity for this course. My only surprise was that they had risked staying so long in an area fully lighted by my burning boat, and with the German trawler unit in close attendance.

4. At that time our flotilla was in the course of fitting ladders up the stern for picking survivors up. Unfortunately neither M.G.B. 77 nor M.G.B. 112 yet had these fitted, otherwise we should all have been picked up. These ladders are invaluable and should be fitted to all Coastal Force craft.

5. After about half an hour M.G.Bs 4 non-swimmers and

myself were picked up by a German trawler. We were well treated, receiving medical attention and hot drinks at once, and were taken to ROTTERDAM. Before leaving the trawler I was able to observe her armament consisted of a gun of about 4in calibre amidships and twin 38mm mountings in raised platforms forward and aft. She had been built in GERMANY in 1939.

6. The same day we were taken to the German Dulag at WILHELMSHAVEN arriving 1000 28th February. My interrogation was not severe as German intelligence about Coastal forces seemed very good. I was shown a copy of Nore Operational Memoranda. The Germans showed great contempt for our having petrol tanks above the water-line. It is the universal opinion of every Coastal Force officer in captivity that small Coastal Force craft should have tanks below the water-line, more armament and should save weight by cutting out all accommodation, which is quite redundant in view of the range of the craft.

7. On 12th March I was taken to the Naval camp Marlag und Milag Nord, at WESTERTINKT near BREMEN where I at once interested myself in the problem of escaping.

8. Early in April Mr Hobbs, Sutcliffe and myself set out on a wire-cutting scheme of Hobbs'. Unfortunately we had to turn back as it was not dark enough nor was it ever dark enough before summer. In December, however, Mr. Hobbs together with Messrs. Freeman, Hardy & Willis did use this scheme with complete success, but were all subsequently apprehended near the DUTCH frontier.

9. From June till August I was engaged on digging a tunnel called 'Mabel'. This tunnel, a major camp effort was conceived and its digging organized by Hercule Poirot. Unfortunately it was discovered just before completion.

10. In September Mr. Sydney Horler took over the escape organization. It had always been the custom in the camp to

have a system of patents with regard to methods of getting out of the camp. That is to say anyone who had an idea for getting out had to tell it to the Escape Officer, but was then given priority in its use.

11. In November I 'patented' a scheme for escape, which I was lucky enough to be able to use twice, as the Germans failed to find the method out. Every Thursday we were taken up in batches of 40 to a bath-house outside the camp. This bath-house had a lavatory from a changing-room with an outside door that was kept locked. My scheme was to wait for a wet Thursday, when the guards used to come into the changing-room instead of patrolling outside, and then pick the lock of the lavatory door.

12. The weak point of the scheme lay in the fact that we were carefully counted several times both before and after bathing. As it was impossible to falsify the count I decided to rely on German corruption. The guards stood to get 3 weeks arrest for letting a prisoner escape and it occurred to me that rather than get this, the guards themselves would, on finding the shortage at the bath-house, rush the party through the main gates, tell the Feldwebel of the watch that all was well and hope the escape would never be traced to them. This line of reasoning in fact held good for both occasions.

13. Also both times my absence was 'covered' for 2 'appels' in the Camp, which gave me 24 hours start. This was organized by Mr. Horler and was done by juggling with the sick who were counted in bed in their barracks. It was comparatively easy to get one man to be counted sick in 2 different rooms. On both occasions, too, I received very considerable help from Mr. Sherlock Holmes, who used to take my gear to the bath-house and act as my support party there.

14. The greatest difficulty of an escape from Marlag lay in getting out of the area. Being near the coast the district is littered with troops, and furthermore, since it appears to be

a regular lane for British bombers, there are usually 'Land-wacht', (the German Home Guards) on the look-out for parachutists. The rail communication consisted of a small gauge railway from TARMSTEDT some 2 miles from the camp, which, stopping every few kilometres, takes $1\frac{1}{2}$ hours to cover the 29kms to BREMEN. Believing that the bold and obvious course would always be best with Germans, I decided that to catch the mid-day train in from the local station would be the safest, simply because of the inherent improbability of a prisoner doing any such thing.

15. On my first attempt on Thursday, 9th December, I went in full British uniform with a Naval Identity card in Russian characters, suggesting that I was Sb.Lt. Ivan Bagerov of the Royal Bulgarian Navy. I also took with me a letter from the First Secretary of the Bulgarian Legation saying that I was 'employed on liaison duties of a technical nature involving me in much travel, and since I had but little knowledge of German, the usual benevolent assistance of all German Officials were solicited on my behalf'. Both letter and pass were made by Mr. Rembrandt, who had for over 2 years done all our forging. The character part of Ivan Bagerov and the writing of the letter in German were both done by Mr. Edgar Wallace, to whose ingenuity in creating escape characters and knowledge of languages for writing letters the camp owes an incalculable debt. For the journey into BREMEN I had to have a different rig since our uniform was well known on the local line. I travelled that part therefore with grey flannels over my Naval trousers and black silk covers over my naval greatcoat buttons, as a Danish Electrician Christof Lindholm. I had a 'volaüfig Ausweiss' and a chit telling me to report back to Bremen Hospital that day. My story was that I had been injured in a recent raid and evacuated to the country to rest my nerves.

16. Thursday, 9th December, I made a successful break from the bath-house and walked to the station carrying a bag containing change of clothes, razor, soap, bread, chocolate and Turkish cigarettes. Every item in the bag was marked

with the name of Bagerov and the chocolate and soap were stamped with some Russian hieroglyphics. On the way to the station I went into a wood and bandaged my head in order further to substantiate my Danish story for the local train. Just outside the station I was stopped by the village policeman, but succeeded in convincing him of my identity.

17. Travelling in a non-smoker full of shopping wives, I had no trouble on the journey into BREMEN, leaving at 11.50 a.m. and getting in at 1.20 p.m. On arrival at the Klein-bahn (Park Bahnhof) I went into the lavatory and burnt my set of Danish papers, discarded my grey flannels and button covers, and, to look more Bulgarian, darkened my eyes and moustache.

18. On arrival at Bremen Hauptbahnhof I was ignorant as to whether to use the civilian or Wehrmacht Eingang. I therefore approached the Military Policeman on duty, produced my papers and asked for help. He was very courteous and sent an assistant who bought me a 3rd class ticket for Lübeck, indicated the time and platform of my train and then took me to the waiting-room and ordered me a beer.

19. I travelled on the 1553 from BREMEN to HAMBURG, arriving at the latter at about 1830. In the waiting-room where I ate the Stamm I was eyed very curiously by a member of the Afrika Korps. I then caught the 2030 to LÜBECK. In my compartment were a Hauptgefreiter and a civilian both quite young. Despite the presence of a strange third party in uniform, they complained a lot of the bombing and were also saying that the evacuation was un-fairly worked in that party members did not have to take refugees, while no one else could call their houses their own. They both advised me that it would be unwise to spend the night in such a big town as LÜBECK and said that the best place would be the waiting-room of a station called Bad Kleinen, the junction for Wismar. Before I could refuse the civilian bought me a supplementary ticket

to go there, so I decided to go to STETTIN first and then return to LÜBECK.

20. After a good night at BAD KLEINEN, I caught a train at about 0500 which brought me to STETTIN about 1330 but an inspection of the free harbour showed no Swedish ships. During the whole day my Naval uniform had caused no comment.

21. In the evening I caught the last train out of STETTIN travelling 2nd class as an experiment in the direction of LÜBECK, intending to spend the night at NEU BRANDENBURG. At this latter, I was just going into the Civilian waiting-room when a Military Policeman caught me and ushered me into the 'Rote Kreuz' Wehrmacht Unterkunft. Here I was given a bowl of soup and ersatz coffee. I did not sleep very well, however, as there was a German Naval officer and about a dozen ratings at the same table. It seemed incredible that they should fail to recognize the uniform of the enemy they had been fighting for over 4 years.

22. Next day I caught the first train at about 6 a.m. to LÜBECK arriving at 10.50. On arrival I went to a hotel and had a shave, followed by a very good Stamm lunch. After lunch I searched the docks and located two small Swedish steamers moored alongside the halbinsel. Still believing that my bluff policy would pay, I succeeded in walking straight through the dock-gates without being challenged by the sentry and boarded the nearest ship. She was a small coaster of about 300 tons and her Steward after ascertaining the state of the coal bunkers from the Engineer advised me to board the other ship astern, as this latter was due to sail the same day. For some time I demurred as I was not anxious to leave my place of comparative safety. At length he persuaded me, and as I went on deck the other ship sailed. Had I been even one minute sooner, nothing could have stopped me since she had been cleared and the Steward had apparently helped prisoners before.

23. I went back therefore to my Steward friend in the first ship and he told me that she was too small to hide me until Monday, but that if I returned then he would take me. There was nothing for it but to go, and on the way out of the docks I got picked up by the guard.

24. The soldier took me to the Duty Officer, who took me to H.Q. Both my person and baggage were searched, but they were unable to find anything wrong with me. I was then taken to the Wasserschultzpolizei, who found my papers had been forged and handed me over to the military after informing my camp. I am certain from my cross-examination that no effort is made outside the immediate area to apprehend or follow up escaping P.O.W.s. I imagine that the reason for this is that the numbers who do actually succeed in getting clear without giving themselves away is not worth the vast amount of extra police work involved in apprehending them.

25. After two days, during which time I was well treated by the local military, two guards arrived from the camp on Monday 13th December, to escort me back. We left LÜBECK at about 1600 and arrived at HAMBURG about 1800. On arrival there, the guards refused to go on any further as it would be impossible to get through BREMEN that night, and they took the view that Hamburg was so ruined that no one could conceivably ever want to bomb it again. I was therefore taken to the Hamburg Militär intersuchungs gefängniss, where I passed a not too comfortable night. One interesting fact I was able to observe, however, was that about a third of the prisoners were German naval ratings. In view of the fact that the greater number of the prisoners there are, I understand, long term men (there are two British naval ratings there for sabotage) it occurred to me that this might be significant.

26. On Tuesday, 14th December, we had quite an exciting journey back to the camp. The day before there had been widespread raids on North Germany. In fact I overheard someone say in the district train that the whole of the old

147

part of KIEL was in flames. One stick of bombs too had fallen on the line between WILHELMSBURG and HAR-BURG, cutting all direct communication from HAM-BURG Hauptbahnhof to the west. We therefore had to take the local train to HARBURG and then make our way as best we could to WILHELMSBURG. Outside HAR-BURG station there was a crowd of several hundred people trying to board any conveyance that came along. No emergency bus service had been arranged although it was then some twenty hours after the raid took place. At first the authorities tried to keep our train load at the barrier but after a short time the crowd tired of this and burst through. Every available seat in every car was immediately seized by strapping young soldiers and the whole route to WIL-HELMBURG was littered with old ladies humping their few pathetic belongings along. Although everyone knew I was British there was no antipathy displayed, in fact I was shown every consideration. After this, no further adven-tures befell us before we arrived back at the camp late that evening.

27. On the local train I met three young Russians. One of them spoke good German. He was aged 22 and had been taken prisoner $2\frac{1}{2}$ years before outside Leningrad. Unlike most of his compatriots he had been living in a small commando and working on the land. He said his treatment had not been too bad and that he had got enough to eat. He wel-comed me as an ally and insisted on my taking five ciga-rettes from a box of a hundred he had with him.

28. For this escape attempt, I got 10 days arrest. During my spell in the 'bunker' there was a complete change in our guard personnel, all the younger men being sent away to man the West Wall and their places being taken by men of the 40–50 age group. Many of these had only been back in uniform for about a fortnight. Their morale was con-siderably worse than that of the younger men and most of them were anti-government. None of them, however, held out any hopes of it being possible to do anything about it, owing to the efficiency and ruthlessness of the police. As a

result of many talks with Germans, I have the strongest views to the effect that the quickest way to soften their resistance prior to an invasion would be to offer them some definite assurance of a tolerable life after the war is over. Their fear of the Russians is so much greater than their fear of us that they would be very willing to believe any such promises, which might well be the instrument of saving many allied lives, when the invasion comes.

29. On my release from the bunker on 26th December, I immediately began to prepare for another attempt. Since I speak Swedish, I resolved to go as a Swedish merchant service officer, who had been wounded while the *Arnold Bratt* of Gothenburg was discharging at BREMEN. I took with me a Temporary Swedish passport and a letter from my consul urging that 'since in my stay in Germany I had suffered so much pain, both physical and mental, every effort be made to make my journey home a pleasant one'. As usual Mr. Edgar Wallace translated this letter into German officialese while Dr. Crippen, a very fine draughtsman from Italy, did the forging. I understand that one of Dr. Crippen's clients got home successfully and it is to the quality of his work that I owe my safety. There is no trouble to which he will not go to help escapers with their papers.

30. For my other preparations I bought a merchant service cap badge and set of buttons and also a set of civilian buttons to the back of which I sewed rings. With split pins inside the greatcoat I could therefore change my coat from a service into a civilian one in rather under two minutes and I had only to remove the badge from my cap to have a plain peaked cap such as German civilians often wear. I also secured a German despatch case in which to carry my food and change of clothing. As previously, I put my name of Sven Lindholm inside every article of clothing. Money, we were able to buy in the camp against our camp marks. Mr. Sherlock Holmes again gave me invaluable assistance including forging a camp pass to use in the vicinity of the camp. Finally since I was likely to be recognized by the

local constable and in the train, Mr. Boris Karloff gave me a magnificent and very disgusting make-up consisting of cardboard scabs coloured with Friars Balsam and stuck on with a gooey concoction of violin beeswax and surgical spirit. Furthermore a large portion of my hair and one eyebrow were shaved off and sticking plaster put over them.

31. I had to delay my departure for three weeks before I could get a suitable occasion, finally making my getaway at 12.15 on Thursday, 10th February. I walked down the road in a heavy snowstorm meeting nobody and half-way to the station, entered a wood where I intended to wait for the evening train. During a 7-hour lie-up it snowed continuously and my feet got colder and colder both literally and metaphorically. I mention this only because it may perhaps interest future escapers that whereas the first escape is an exciting adventure, the second is an intolerably dull slog, but one with far greater chances of success.

32. At 1930 I left the wood and walked to the station catching the 2003. There was no patrol as I had been led to expect and I arrived at BREMEN without incident at 2130. There was no train out of BREMEN before 0405, so I slept in the waiting-room. In the middle of the night a very efficient station policeman asked to see my papers and expressed himself quite satisfied with them. This and a similar occasion in DANZIG Hptbnhf were the only two occasions when I was asked for my papers during more than 1,000 kilometres of train travel. At this stage of my journey I had the civilian buttons on my coat.

33. At about 0200 the sirens went and I had to troop down into the shelter. Everybody was perfectly quiet and orderly and no bombs fell. Some prosperous families seemed to have private rooms in the shelter. As soon as the alarm was over, I went up to buy my ticket. Having already passed the police I made a fuss buying my ticket for LÜBECK, mispronouncing it and giving the wrong sum of money. I did this so that the girl should remember the incident when

the balloon went up at 0900 as by that time I intended to be well past LÜBECK and wanted to concentrate any hue and cry there.

34. I caught the 0405 E-Zug from BREMEN and removed my scabs in the lavatory. On arrival in HAMBURG I changed platforms and got on to the LÜBECK train which moved off at once. The train spent ten minutes in LÜBECK from 0755 till 0805 during which time I bought a ticket to ROSTOCK. I was thus well clear of any possible trouble when I was reported missing at 0900 appel. Changing at BAD KLEINEN and BUTZOW, I arrived at ROSTOCK at about 1100 and set out at once to search the docks. These were empty except for one German steamer.

35. Bomb damage in ROSTOCK is extensive but confined to the residential and shopping areas. The Neptune shipyard, which appears to have greatly increased in size, was untouched as was a small Daimler-Benz factory in the neighbourhood.

36. Catching the WARNEMUNDE–BERLIN express at about 1600 I went to GUSTROW where I dined and then on to NEU BRANDENBURG where I spent the night, catching the first morning train into STETTIN, where I arrived at 0900 on Saturday, 12th February. The main station, which had been standing on my previous visit, was this time completely flat. Apart from this I saw no new damage. Particularly on the east bank of the river, there were many extensive and highly camouflaged factory targets that would be the better for a few bombs. There is also an aerodrome just by FINKENWALDE Station from which I saw Me 109 and 110s, Junker 88s and several other types of plane take off and land. The runway is parallel to the railway line and about 200 yards from it. FINKENWADE is the first station east of STETTIN.

37. A search of the free harbour failed to reveal any Swedish ships and at 1500, on completion of my search, there

occurred an accident which very nearly finished my attempt. When removing the hair from my temple, I had slightly cut myself. On going into a pub to have a late lunch, I inadvertently washed the scab off. Not knowing anything was wrong I ordered a drink, and was sitting reading the paper when the proprietor asked me if I knew that I was pouring with blood. I of course rushed back to the lavatory to repair the damage and was followed by the proprietor, who assisted me. When finished, he asked me out of pure politeness who I was, and on being told that I was a Swede, he broke into fluent Swedish and said that he had lived in Sweden for ten years. My Swedish was not good enough for this, and after keeping my end up for a couple of minutes I left hurriedly leaving my drink unfinished and the proprietor very puzzled. I felt that it was only a matter of time before he should inform the police, so dropping into a public lavatory by the wayside to change my buttons and put on my merchant service cap badge, I booked a ticket for DANZIG and caught the very first train. I was out of STETTIN within half an hour of the occurrence of the incident and never knew if the police were informed.

38. Arriving at BELGARD about 1800, I stopped and had dinner. I was joined at my table by five Frenchmen in the smart green uniform of the so-called Freiwilligers. They assured me that they had all been called up for forced labour, lived in conditions approximating to those of prisoners and hated it. Their morale was excellent and one of them electrified me by saying in a loud voice that 'ces sales boches sont haïts partout'. As a neutral I was unable to join them in these sentiments, much as I was longing to. At 2000 I caught a train on to KUSTRIN where I spent a very comfortable night in the waiting-room. It would appear to be always safe to spend nights in the waiting-rooms of wayside stations, provided that one has a ticket.

39. The next day being Sunday, I was not anxious to proceed to DANZIG, as I was not sure whether there would be enough people around the docks to cover my movements. I therefore took a train on to STOLP, where I spent the day.

In the morning I went to High Mass. The church was packed to capacity and I was surprised at the large number of young men in uniform who were there. The sermon, however, was entirely political and of irreproachable Nazi content. In the evening I caught the last train into DANZIG, arriving at about 1800. I trudged around for a couple of hours in the dark trying to find shelter for the night, and then took a train out to GUTENHAFEN, which I thought might be safer than the main station. In this, however, I was clearly wrong as every train brought loads of sailors back from leave in DANZIG, and there were several Naval Police there to keep order. I saw no trace of drunkenness among them. In view of the weakness of German beer this is not to be wondered at.

40. Just before midnight I caught the last train back to DANZIG and spent the night in the main waiting-room. My papers were examined by the police but they readily accepted my explanation that I had arrived too late to contact the Swedish consulate or to secure other accommodation. I had taken the precaution of looking up the consul's address and telephone number beforehand.

41. My position next morning was that I had only 6 Rms left. It was therefore essential that I should board a ship of some sort that day or else get help and accommodation from the French. A long search of the docks showed no Swedish ships, but two Danes, the *Scandia* and *Thor*. These were both loading grain on the west side of the peninsula that divides the two arms of the Free Harbour. A sentry patrolled the quayside, but it seemed that it might be possible to go down the east side of the peninsula which was unguarded anyway by day, hide up in the warehouses and then approach the ship's gangway from the seaward side of the spit after dark. Before doing this I contacted three separate groups of French P.O.W. workmen. All were sympathetic but none had any offers of food or shelter.

42. I therefore finished my money in a last big feed and hid myself in a narrow alley-way between two warehouses at

the end of the spit, just before dark. While waiting, I burnt all my papers, since they would certainly not be able to cover my movements should I fail to get on board unobserved. I chose 2100 as the time to go aboard, as this should be just after the last change of guard before moonrise. It was still distressingly light as I approached the gangway, but luckily the sentry was using a torch, and at the extreme end of his beat its rays were not sufficiently strong to pick me up, while its use meant that he would be unable to see in the dark as I could.

43. With the combination of factors outlined above, I succeeded in getting aboard the Danish ship *Scandia* and going down into the boiler room, I met Stoker Amundsen, who told me that the ship was due to take grain down to LÜBECK and then coal to DENMARK. This was hardly what I wanted but seemed better than nothing, so I accepted his offer to hide me in the coal and give me food and water.

44. The next five days were spent in complete darkness and the only thing to mark the passage of time was the arrival of my $\frac{1}{2}$ pint of water and 3 sandwiches every evening at 8 p.m. Great caution had to be observed as Amundsen was anxious that no other member of the crew should know that I was there. By day, when the trimmers were at work in the main bunkers, I used to lie on a narrow ledge in the 'tween deck bunkers, coming down to sleep on the coal at night. We sailed at 0600 on Wednesday, 16th February, and arrived at LÜBECK at 1200 on Friday, 18th February. On Saturday 19th, the ship bunkered. Late that evening Amundsen came down and told me that instead of taking coal to Denmark as anticipated, the ship was due to return empty to KÖNIGSBERG to load grain for BREMEN, going from the latter with briquettes home. Since this would involve a further fortnight in pitch darkness to take me back to the doors of the camp, and would also involve Amundsen in much further risk, I decided to leave the ship in LÜBECK, which I knew well enough to find my way round in the dark and endeavour to find another ship.

After five days in coal my state was such that I would have to be aboard another ship by first light or I would certainly be picked up.

45. On going up on deck, I found that there was no sentry on deck but the whole area was floodlit and there was a sentry in the doorway of the elevator. Luckily it was a very cold night, and as it drew on towards midnight the sentry tended to spend more and more time inside the elevator. Profiting by one of these moments, I jumped ashore and succeeded in gaining cover unobserved.

46. Going north up the west bank of the river, I soon smelt timber and climbed a low wall into the timber yards. I found one large steamer with a deck cargo and bearing a Swedish name. It was the sort of night when visibility is deceptive. I could hear a sentry moving about but could never see him. I therefore took off my shoes and crept aboard. There was no port of registry marked on her lifeboats, but there were lights in a cabin. I approached the door and was disappointed to hear Finnish conversation.

47. Continuing my stocking-footed prowl I entered a yard with an M-class sweeper in it. There was no sign of life, but I saw no reason to board her. There were no other ships on the west bank of the river. The whole area seems to be very ill-guarded and saboteurs equipped with time charges, could easily cause immense damage in the dock area.

48. Whilst crossing the main bridge over the river, the sirens went and I spent an hour underneath a lorry in case it would be dangerous to be seen moving about during an alarm. I was pitch black and without papers and any challenge would have been fatal. Continuing my search down the east bank of the river I came to the SVEA line quay, at which I hoped I might find a mail ship bound for GOTH-ENBURG. There was a large steamer there and no sentry •on the gangway. I boarded her, but could find no clue as to

her name. I entered the charthouse, but it was dark and I had no matches. Then I went aft and hauled down her ensign, but could not see what nationality she was. The German sentry who by this time was back at his post watched me do this, but obviously thought I was a member of the crew. Finally I heard snores from the galley and found the nightwatchman asleep. By his side was one of those peculiar Finnish knives, which from a year spent in a Finnish four-masted barque, I recognized at once. Shortly afterwards the nightwatchman came out and accosting him in the dark I asked him the ship's name, time of sailing and destination. He told me readily enough that she was the *Canopus* and due to sail for STOCKHOLM at 7 a.m. or rather under two hours' time with a cargo of oranges. He then asked who I was. I told him the German customs.

49. It was by then so late that this ship seemed to be my last chance. I found my way down to the engine room and there met a stoker. I told him I was British and said I was anxious to go to STOCKHOLM. He pointed out, naturally enough, that our countries were at war, but said he liked the British. I then told him of my year in the Finnish mercantile marine and asked him if he knew any of my friends from MARIEHAMN. Finally since he would be risking his life by taking me I offered him the sum of £200 for my passage. Finally he put me underneath the boilers. I need hardly say that my 2½ days were rather too warm to be pleasant, but a most thorough German Police search never thought of looking there. In two out of three watches, I was able to have a manhole to the stokehold open and was given vast plates of pea soup and porridge. In the third watch the stokers were unreliable, and I had to be sealed in. It then grew stifling but by keeping my nose right down in the bilge I managed to get a current of fresh air.

50. We docked in STOCKHOLM about 1500 on Tuesday, 22nd February, but at the stokers' request I remained on board till after dark, when I went ashore and contacted the British Consul-General. I was only detained by the Swedish police for one night and received every kindness from

them. It took five baths to get the coal off me and my clothes had to be destroyed. I was set free at midday on Wednesday, 23rd February.

51. No report would be complete without mention of the extraordinary hospitality I have received from members of the Legation and Consulate.

52. *Conclusions.*

I. The Swedish route is a very good one, particularly for anyone keen on the sea and ships.

II. In Marlag and Milag Nord, more intelligence is needed about this route, and it is suggested that it be sent from Stockholm, since that would involve so much less delay.

III. Since it is so heartening to a camp to know that people have got clear, it is suggested that the names of arrivals home be included in Overseas Service broadcasts. This would tell the Germans nothing they do not already know and would serve to stimulate camp escaping activity, since most camps receive the B.B.C.

IV. Since the days of long journeys on foot are over, it is suggested that Identity cards and ration cards be sent to camps. It is understood that this has been done in some cases but none have ever reached Marlag (O).

POSTSCRIPT:–

After being reunited with my family, I reported at the Admiralty at 10 o'clock the following morning to find myself in for a hectic week of debriefing in that I was seen by everyone from the First Sea Lord and the Head of N.I.D. to Admiral Commanding Submarines, who wanted to know all about the crews of the submarines *Seal*, *Shark* and *Swordfish* which had been sunk in the Kattegat at the time of the Norwegian invasion. The Foreign Office too, wanted to see me and I lunched with R. A. Butler who, at the time, was Secretary of State for Education and to whom my father was P.P.S. On all political interviews I stressed my opinion, which came out in my report in Stockholm to the effect that a policy of unconditional surrender could only lengthen the war at a cost of many extra Allied lives. But it was made clear to me that Churchill, Roosevelt and Stalin had made up their minds firmly on this point and no-one could hope to make any mileage out of raising the issue.

I then started a four week period of leave during which, aided by the Red Cross, who had all the addresses of next-of-kin, I threw cocktail parties both in London and in Glasgow for the relations of those still in the Camp since I felt I owed it to fate as the least I could do, and that it probably would help them to see someone just back who was obviously fit and well and could give a happy account of life over there. I also called on a lot of people individually who could not get to either of the parties. One was the doctor father of a young sub-lieutenant who had richly earned a D.S.O. as one of the four survivors of the miniature submarine attacks on the *Tirpitz*. He came straight to the point over the soup saying, 'either my son is out of his mind or he is writing in code. Is he out of his mind?' I replied, 'No, he is not out of his mind.' 'Good', said the doctor, 'that is all I needed to know, say no more.' And from that moment on we discussed everything other than the war. Another rather pathetic interview was with the mother of a Merchant Service Engineer who was the one person in our camp who had gone over to the Germans, having been taken to a luxury camp safely outside Berlin where he was sent off on recruitment commissions round the various camps. The poor chap obviously suffered from *folie de grandeur* since he was always talking big about 'his mother's friend the Duchess' and similar personages, but when his mother turned up, she was a very nice cockney charlady. Happily at that time I did not know he had defected but merely thought he had been posted to another camp as otherwise it would have been too embarrassing to see her. After the war he was condemned to death along with Lord Haw-Haw and others but this sentence was commuted to life imprisonment when it was shown that he could not have given away our tunnel 'Mabel'. I would sooner though, not recall his name in the hopes that anonymity has overtaken him somewhere.

I then went for a week to Mull before taking a brief course prior to being sent out as a N.I.D. staff lecturer, since it was not policy to expose escaped prisoners to the risk of recapture and obviously my most useful role was briefing Naval invasion forces on German interrogation techniques, urging them, in the event of capture to try and escape before reaching the camp and getting behind barbed wire. This tour had the enormous advantage to me of enabling me to see at first-hand the way of life in almost every unit of the Navy from Fleet Air Arm to submarines. I even lectured round the fleet in Scapa Flow and, with the connivance of my C.O. back in Beaconsfield, managed to get lost aboard the aircraft carrier *Glorious* on one of her North Cape *Tirpitz* strikes.

In October and with the European war drawing to its close, it was proposed to send me out on a similar mission to the Far East which I sought to decline since obviously the conditions were completely different and I had no knowledge of jungle warfare. So instead I was offered a chance to join the Falkland Island Dependency Survey, the forerunner of the modern British Antarctic Survey, as an assistant geographer and meteorologist in charge of dogs. This I very naturally accepted since it was a place to which I had always wanted to go.

After the war it was not long before John Wells started to organise Marleg Reunion evenings which have always been very well attended since nothing has kept people together more firmly than sharing camp life for many months and in some cases, years. Although after 40 years time has inevitably taken its toll, we still usually muster 30 to 40 people and of those mentioned in this book, Frank Jackson, Roy Eccleston, Jim Prior and Bill Hussey still usually attend.

Thirty-seven years later, after I had opened my home here to the public, Bill Hussey re-forged all my documents, as they had been at the time, to go on display in a special cabinet in the Archive Room. The only material difference is that whereas then he could produce a typewritten letter freehand using a 2B pencil, he did find that this was now beyond him and had actually to use a typewriter. This, when you think of it, is an amazing tribute to how good his original work must have been.

About the Author

David James was born on Christmas day 1919, and educated at Summer Fields, Oxford and at Eton. At the age of 17, tired of school life, he persuaded his father to let him leave early and sign on instead for a year as an apprentice in the Finnish four-masted barque *Viking*. He went in this from Copenhagen where he joined her, to East London, South Africa with timber in 79 days, in ballast to Port Victoria in Australia in 24 days (an average speed of nearly 10 knots from port to port), and then after five weeks loading, back to England via Cape Horn in 116 days to Falmouth and four days on to London where he signed off.

On his return he accompanied his father on a trip to observe the Spanish Civil War in which he was more nearly killed by a sniper through incautiously showing himself than he ever was in his own war! There then followed a year at Oxford which was of course, completely over-shadowed by the approach of September, 1939.

After the events covered by the book, he went as related, to the Antarctic for 18 months where he greatly enjoyed the sledging and became extremely attached to his huskies. When he got back he spent three months acting as A.D.C. to the retiring Governor of the Falkland Islands in Port Stanley and then took passage home as a watch-keeper aboard the survey ship *William Scoresby* where, on arrival in Plymouth, his naval career came to an end.

Very luckily, Ealing Studios were just about to film 'Scott of the Antarctic' and he got a job as Polar Advisor which took him back to the Antarctic with the well-known photographer, Osmund Borrodaile, for background shots. From there he went to Jungfraujoch where at 11,500 ft., a film unit together with John Mills and James Robertson Justice, took sequences on the upper reaches of the longest glacier in Europe masquerading as the Beardmore Glacier by which route Captain Scott reached the South Pole. Then after a short break in Mull, it was off to Norway and the Hardanger Jokul, near Finse, on the Oslo–Bergen line, the largest flat ice-cap in Europe to simulate the polar plateau. Then four months of 1948 were spent sewing up the loose ends of the film on the floor in Ealing.

His next commission was to write the definitive life of Field Marshal Lord Roberts who gave him a trip around the Indian Mutiny battlefields; right round the North West Frontier and up to Kabul. But by then it was time to quit wandering and on May 20th, 1950, he married the Honourable Jacquetta Digby who bore him four sons and two daughters.

After some years publishing in London, he became Conservative M.P. for Brighton Kemp Town but in 1964, he lost it by a narrow majority of seven votes after seven recounts and thus found himself out in the wilderness again. He recalls that night as being considerably worse than the night that he was captured. However, in 1970, he was back once again as M.P for North Dorset. He retired in 1979 owing to the increasing and conflicting pressures of opening his home, Torosay Castle on the Island of Mull, to the public and carrying through a thorough programme of restoration. There he and his wife now live, seeing the place get more lovely and the number of visitors more numerous as each year passes.

On going back to Torosay, which had always been his ultimate intention from schooldays, he changed his name to David Guthrie-James because Torosay was a Guthrie property which he inherited from his mother through his grandparents and great-granduncle who had moved to Mull from Angus in 1865.